T0339667

Cambridge Elements ≡

Elements in Leadership
edited by
Ronald Riggio
Claremont McKenna College
Susan Murphy
University of Edinburgh

Founding Editor
Georgia Sorenson
University of Cambridge

THERE IS MORE THAN ONE WAY TO LEAD

The Charismatic, Ideological, and Pragmatic (CIP) Theory of Leadership

Samuel T. Hunter
University of Nebraska, Omaha

Jeffrey B. Lovelace
University of Virginia

CAMBRIDGE
UNIVERSITY PRESS

CAMBRIDGE
UNIVERSITY PRESS

University Printing House, Cambridge CB2 8BS, United Kingdom

One Liberty Plaza, 20th Floor, New York, NY 10006, USA

477 Williamstown Road, Port Melbourne, VIC 3207, Australia

314–321, 3rd Floor, Plot 3, Splendor Forum, Jasola District Centre, New Delhi – 110025, India

103 Penang Road, #05–06/07, Visioncrest Commercial, Singapore 238467

Cambridge University Press is part of the University of Cambridge.

It furthers the University's mission by disseminating knowledge in the pursuit of education, learning, and research at the highest international levels of excellence.

www.cambridge.org
Information on this title: www.cambridge.org/9781108793216
DOI: 10.1017/9781108883795

© Samuel T. Hunter and Jeffrey B. Lovelace 2022

First published 2022

A catalogue record for this publication is available from the British Library.

ISBN 978-1-108-79321-6 Paperback
ISSN 2631-7789 (online)
ISSN 2631-7788 (print)

There Is More Than One Way to Lead

The Charismatic, Ideological, and Pragmatic (CIP) Theory of Leadership

Elements in Leadership

DOI: 10.1017/9781108883795
First published online: June 2022

Samuel T. Hunter
University of Nebraska, Omaha

Jeffrey B. Lovelace
University of Virginia

Author for correspondence: Samuel T. Hunter, samuelhunter@unomaha.edu

Abstract: The charismatic, ideological, and pragmatic (CIP) theory of leadership has emerged as a novel framework for thinking about the varying ways leaders can influence followers. The theory is based on the principle of equifinality or the notion that there are multiple pathways to the same outcome. Researchers of the CIP theory have proposed that leaders are effective by engaging in one, or a mix, of the three leader pathways: the charismatic approach focused on an emotionally evocative vision, an ideological approach focused on core beliefs and values, or a pragmatic approach focused on an appeal of rationality and problem-solving. Formation of pathways and unique follower responses are described. The more than fifteen years of empirical work investigating the theory are summarized, and the theory is compared and contrasted to other commonly studied and popular frameworks of leadership. Strengths, weaknesses, and avenues for future investigation of the CIP theory are discussed.

Keywords: Leadership, Charismatic, Ideological, Pragmatic, CIP, Pathways, Equifinality

ISBNs: 9781108793216 (PB), 9781108883795 (OC)
ISSNs: 2631-7789 (online), 2631-7788 (print)

Contents

1 Introduction and Overview

In late 2016, Elon Musk found himself stuck in traffic on a packed Los Angeles highway. Frustrated, he sent a series of tweets stating "Traffic is driving me nuts. Am going to build a tunnel boring machine and just start digging . . . ." So began the ambitious plans for the Hyperloop, a series of underground tunnels designed to get people from Los Angeles to San Francisco, a span of about 350 miles, in 35 minutes. Such plans were happening simultaneously with efforts to develop SpaceX, the first private space travel company as well as his more well-known company Tesla that has shaken the Detroit auto industry with its focus on stylish, high-performing electric vehicles. His entrepreneurial efforts have not been limited to only these aspiring projects, nor have all of his projects resulted in resounding success. Yet, even with a consideration of this sample of projects, change and a visionary future orientation help define the Elon Musk approach to leading.

In November 2018, more than 20,000 Google employees participated in a mass walkout in protest of several issues, including the handling of sexual harassment allegations. The effort was co-led by two employees at Google including the prominent voice of Meredith Whittaker. Whittaker has been a strong advocate for focusing on core values at Google, where she has spoken out against developing artificial intelligence (AI)-based military drones as well as other issues surrounding AI and ethics. Her strong beliefs clashed with Google's upper leadership, and she ultimately left the organization to serve as co-founder of the organization "AI Now" that centers on ethics and responsibility in the AI space. There is little denying Whittaker's brilliance as a scientist and even less room to deny her commitment as a leader to her core beliefs and values in the technology arena.

Many of us have sent samples to a lab to learn more about our roots and trace our ancestry. We have Anne Wojcicki and her company 23andMe to thank for much of that knowledge. Wojcicki is a brilliant innovator, breaking barriers at YouTube and Google. Her approach, however, is quite different from that of Musk and Whittaker, in that she has laid problem-solving, not a future-focused vision or focus on a system of beliefs, as her leadership foundation. In an interview with *Inc.* magazine (Ryan, 2019), she notes, "When we try out new products here, I tell my employees they should assume some things will resonate with people and some things won't . . . . You should be a constant learning machine." As described by Carter (2016) in an interview for the *Wall Street Journal*, "For this CEO . . . pragmatic solutions are a way of life." Wojcicki has an impressive array of successes as a leader, and her approach to getting there has been through a focus on rationality and pragmatism.

These three leaders serve to illustrate contrasting approaches to leading successfully in organizations. Elon Musk with his focus on change and novelty, Meredith Whittaker with her focus on core beliefs and values, and Anne Wojcicki with her pragmatic approach to advancement through problem-solving. What is fundamental to this effort, however, is understanding that despite their differing styles, all three have proven to be highly successful leaders in a similar arena. This trend, moreover, is not unique to Silicon Valley or the technology space. In the civil rights era, three leaders took very different approaches to leading (Bedell-Avers et al., 2009). Booker T. Washington served as a pragmatist, Frederick Douglas as a charismatic visionary, and W. E. B. Du Bois as the ideologue, yet all three collectively led improvements to civil rights. The last three US presidents also contrast each other stylistically, with Barack Obama's charismatic campaign on hope; Donald Trump's focus on an idealized bygone era, seeking to make America "great again"; and Joe Biden's pragmatic focus on listening to scientists and experts as the way forward. Professional and college football coaches (Hunter et al., 2011), world leaders during COVID-19 (Crayne & Medeiros, 2020), and student samples (Hunter et al., 2009; Lovelace & Hunter, 2013) all illustrate an important but often overlooked observation about leadership: there is more than one way to successfully lead people and organizations. In this Element, we explore these three styles of charismatic leadership, ideological leadership, and pragmatic leadership, referred to as the charismatic, ideological, and pragmatic (CIP) theory of leadership.

1.1 Origins of the CIP Theory

Max Weber was a German scientist with expertise in sociology and economics, although interestingly he preferred to see himself as a historian (Burke, 2005; Wren & Bedeian, 2020). Weber heavily influenced a number of scientific domains, including most relevant here the study of management and leadership (1924, 1947). More specifically, he was one of the first leadership scholars to suggest that there were multiple types of forms of authority and influence. The three forms he discussed were charismatic, traditional, and rational. The charismatic influence was linked to exemplary character and heroism; traditional styles of influence were linked to timeworn tradition; and rational influence was based on respecting processes, bureaucracy, standardized approaches, and the positions held by those in those bureaucratic roles. Weber's work laid the foundation for the notion that there are multiple ways to lead and manage others.

Although other researchers have discussed the notion of varying forms of influence and styles of leading (e.g., Hackman & Wageman, 2007), it was Mumford (2006) who formally instantiated the CIP theory. Mumford and colleagues (2020) outline the origins of the CIP theory, and their account is certainly worth a read. Their discussion points to a number of influences shaping the emergence of the framework with two standing out as most influential. The first was Mumford's initial reading of a Benjamin Franklin biography earlier in his career. This initial foray into the life of Franklin led to a qualitative analysis of ten social innovations he led (Mumford, 2002; Mumford & Van Dorn, 2001), and in that work, the seed of an idea was born. Franklin was prolific as an inventor and highly impactful as a leader but was hardly viewed as a charismatic individual. Instead, he led primarily through rational appeals, convincing others to follow through logic and reasoning. The second early influence driving the development of the CIP theory came about through Mumford's early career work with the Department of Defense and the intelligence community. When the terrorist attack occurred in the United States on 9/11, Dr. Mumford and his team set out to examine how such an event could happen drawing on his experiences in the intelligence community as well as his expertise as a researcher. Specifically, he led a group seeking to understand how followers were convinced to participate in these destructive activities. The finding from this work was that destructive leadership took on several forms including most relevant here, the realization that ideological leadership or a focus on beliefs and values was one pathway to substantial outcomes at the individual follower and organizational levels (Mumford et al., 2007).

These observations on leadership emerging from detailed examinations of leaders such as Benjamin Franklin as well as events surrounding 9/11 stood in contrast to the emerging zeitgeist at the time. Namely, leadership was largely dominated by a focus on transformational and charismatic leadership (Bass, 1985; Yukl, 1999). These perspectives emphasized creating a compelling and positively emotion-laden vision for followers. Rather than rejecting the robust findings that transformational and charismatic leadership were quite appealing, Mumford (2006) took a more novel approach. He drew on the work of Weber and suggested that there were multiple pathways to the same outcome and that the charismatic pathway was just one avenue to successful leadership. That is, it was possible for leaders to engage in differing approaches to leading yet still be successful in achieving their goals. Through a large-scale effort involving countless hours of coding more than 200 academic biographies, the foundational principles of the CIP theory of leadership were born.

1.2 Equifinality and Leadership

The key feature that makes the CIP unique is the premise of multiple pathways to the same or similar outcomes. This premise is known as equifinality, a concept emerging from the fields of physics and biology (Von Bertalanffy, 1950). Interestingly, a strong case for equifinality and multiple viable pathways to achievement has been made across a variety of research domains, such as innovative performance, school achievement, and decision-making in social contexts (e.g., Baas et al., 2013; Bledow et al., 2009; Joshi & Knight, 2015; Stuürmer & Simon, 2004). Within the domains of leadership and management, however, there have only been a limited number of applications of the equifinality concept. Hackman and Wageman (2007) recently suggested that equifinality had utility in thinking about leadership but was often missed due to an overreliance on singular (i.e., one best way to lead) approaches. They express a sentiment that echoes the broader criticism of the leadership literature's overreliance on vision-based perspectives like transformational or charismatic leadership (Dinh et al., 2014; Lord et al., 2017; Van Knippenberg & Sitkin, 2013). Furthermore, Ashmos and Huber (1987) as well as Gresov and Drazin (1997) referred to equifinality in the study of organizational systems and management as one of the critical "missed opportunities" (p. 404). Although the leadership and management domains have not fully embraced the concept of equifinality, there are a few important and notable exceptions that are offered later in this Element.

In their work on organizations and systems theory, for example, Katz and Kahn (1978) suggested that equifinality occurs in organizations when "a system can reach the same final state, from different initial conditions and by a variety of different paths" (p. 30). Along similar lines in the strategy literature, Porter (1980) suggested that competitive advantage could be gained via three equally viable strategic approaches: being unique and different, being more narrowly focused on what was done previously, and solving problems across a range of pragmatic cost issues. Relatedly, Miles and colleagues (1978) suggested that organizations could be successful in adapting to change, using differing yet equivalently viable approaches or types that include *defenders* who seek stability via insulation and a narrowed focus, attempting to "achieve strict control of the organization" (p. 551); *prospectors* who emphasize change and for whom "maintaining a reputation as an innovator" (p. 552) was their key to success; and *analyzers* who keep a watchful eye on emerging trends, operating across several product domains, and shifting to solve problems as needed. Perhaps most relevant to our effort is the aforementioned work of Weber (1924, 1947), who suggested that there were three types of legitimizing authorities in the context of managing employees and followers. Thus, we can see that the notion of equifinality has percolated in leadership and organizational thinking for some time now, with the CIP theory formally incorporating the premise into its foundation.

1.3 The CIP Model and Mental Models: How Leader Pathways Are Formed

The macro leadership literature has established that leader decisions differ in situations that involve multiple stimuli in complex and ambiguous situations (Cyert & March, 1963; Finkelstein et al., 2009; Mischel, 1977). It is these critical decisions that are guided by the framework of the leader's sensemaking process, not some set of known optimal actions, that guides successful outcomes. Leaders perceive the same situations in different ways, identify different sets of options to deal with problems, and ultimately vary in how they implement their leadership approach (Barnard, 1938; Hambrick, 1989). We argue that these points parallel the perspective of Mumford and colleagues' conceptualization of their CIP model and fit well within an equifinality approach that requires and allows for an open, complex system with multiple pathways to the same outcome. Thus, by building off the work of Weber (1947) and Mumford (2006), we reconcile the broader leadership literature with more macro perspectives (Hambrick, 2007; Hiller et al., 2011) by explaining that all of these perspectives recognize that differences in the approach of leaders (i.e., their styles of leadership) can be attributed to foundational variance in their leader orientations. Drawing from these perspectives (Finkelstein et al., 2009; Hambrick & Mason, 1984; March & Simon, 1958), we explain that leader orientation is, broadly speaking, the mental framework that guides a leader's view of the world (descriptive mental model) and how they choose to operate within their world as leaders (prescriptive mental model). Visualized in Figure 1, leader orientation is the primary initial pathway differentiator in the model.

1.3.1 Leader Orientation Formation: Descriptive Mental Models

Before turning to the role of mental models in how leaders approach each pathway, it is important to acknowledge that the sensemaking literature is complex, and recent reviews reveal that there is no single agreed-upon definition of the phenomenon (see Brown et al., 2015). In the case of CIP, researchers have taken a mental model perspective on sensemaking whereby leaders reduce equivocality for followers by providing a framework to guide perceptions of both how the world operates (e.g., causes of outcomes) and how the world will be. Thus, leaders are not providing followers with a snapshot of a yet-to-be-discovered truth, but rather offering their "invented" (Brown et al., 2015) perspective as dictated by life experience (Weick, 1995).

Stated in the framing of mental models as sensemaking mechanisms, how a leader views their world will ultimately shape how they will attempt to

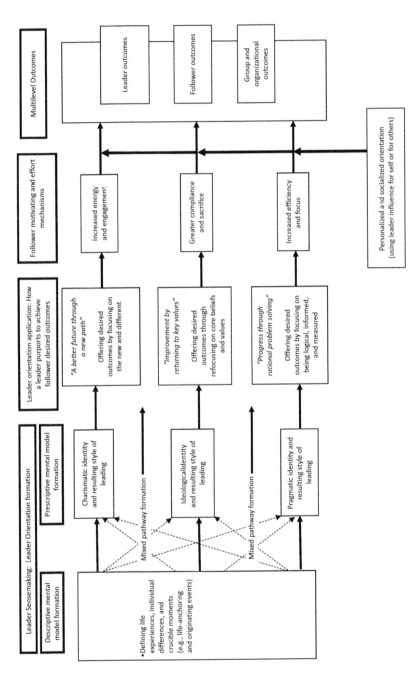

Figure 1 CIP model of leadership

operate and function as leaders within that world (Strange & Mumford, 2005). More directly, leaders are "active authors" (Brown et al., 2015, p. 267) offering their view of how and why events occur. Key or crucible life experiences have a strong impact on what a leader sees as the causes and goal linkages of outcomes (Goldvarg & Johnson-Laird, 2001; Janson, 2008) and serve to sculpt their descriptive mental model (Bennis & Thomas, 2002; Hambrick & Mason, 1984; Mumford et al., 2006e; Weick, 1995). Research indicates that a variety of specific experiences influence a leader's cognitive orientation (e.g., Atwater et al., 1999; Day et al., 2014; Hall, 2004; Kotter, 1988). For example, a leader's educational background, developmental experiences in specific functional areas (e.g., pilot training, military experience), and family experiences all influence how leaders vary in their identification of important information to consider and their interpretation of that key information (Finkelstein et al., 2009; Strange & Mumford, 2005; Zaccaro et al., 2018). Thus, the blending of a leader's personal experiences and leadership experiences forms the foundation of a leader's orientation (Gioia & Poole, 1984; Pillemer, 2001; Strange & Mumford, 2002). Central to the CIP model, however, is that each pathway is differentiated by a unique set of experiences (Fromm, 1973; McAdams, 2006; Mobley et al., 1992). That is, leaders who solely utilize a charismatic approach will experience a differing set of life-defining moments than those leaders solely following a pragmatic pathway. Moreover, leaders who have the potential to utilize multiple styles may experience a blend of crucible life events that characterize such approaches.

The case of differentiated life experiences serving as the foundation for varying leader pathways is perhaps best made via consideration of work on life narratives. Specifically, Ligon and colleagues (2008) used a life narrative framework (Anderson & Conway, 1993; Habermas & Bluck, 2000) to investigate the life experiences of 120 historical leaders, observing that each of the three leader pathways began with a series of differing life events or narratives. More specifically, they found that charismatic leaders experienced a greater number of life-redirecting events or life events that involved a fundamental change in an individual's life direction, creating a comfort level with change and ambiguity. Ideological leaders experienced more life-anchoring events or life events that highlighted the importance and function of belief systems when making critical decisions. Pragmatic leaders experienced more analytical originating events or life events that promoted the importance of focusing on empirical information and the immediate nature of problems to find incremental success in addressing challenging situations. In each of these cases, life experiences influenced the information leaders saw as important to making sense of critical events and laid a foundation for the interpretation of future events (Hunter et al., 2011; Lovelace et al., 2019).

Furthermore, integrating with macro strategic leadership, Hambrick and Mason's (1984) original work on upper echelons helps solidity the role that experiences play in shaping a leader's worldview and how that worldview influences important outcomes for organizations. In their paper, Hambrick and Mason (1984) propose several upper echelons characteristics (i.e., executive experience, cognition, and values) that in combination with contextual considerations predict firm strategic choice. For ease of measurement and operationalization, early upper echelons research included multiple observable characteristics (i.e., age, functional tracks, career experiences, education, socioeconomic roots, etc.) as proxies that can be used to tap into differences in CEO and Top Management Team (TMT) cognition and values, which ultimately influence key outcomes for organizations (e.g., strategic choices and performance). The underlying assumption is that observable characteristics shape the upper echelon's life narrative, impacting the individual orientation of executives and the subsequent choices they make for their organizations. As such, integrating with our current framework, the importance of crucible life events for leader orientation has been considered both from a macro and micro leadership perspective.

On the whole, crucible life events and leadership events serve as the foundation for leader orientation formation. These critical life events, in particular key leadership experiences (i.e., events that trigger a reflection on or development of one's self-concept and skill as a leader), are essential to the way a leader views the world around them and subsequently makes sense of future challenges they face in organizations (Hammond et al., 2017). This perspective is also consistent with work by Zaccaro and colleagues (2018) who discuss both early life experiences and developmental experiences as key drivers of leadership capacity. Thus, as the work of Ligon and colleagues (2008) and others demonstrate, different types of key events support the adoption of differing leadership pathways.

1.3.2 Leader Orientation Formation: Prescriptive Mental Models

In contrast to a descriptive mental model that depicts how the world operates, a leader's prescriptive mental model represents how the leader believes the world *could be* and is derived largely from reflection on their descriptive mental model (Hunter et al., 2011; Mumford, 2006). In other words, a leader's prescriptive mental model represents the formation of the leader's orientation or approach to leading and, as noted by Brown and colleagues (2015), is most often manifest in sensemaking through discourse or how a leader tells others the world can be. A leader's orientation is the core of a leader's cognitive lens as it drives how they analyze and make decisions in uncertain conditions (Bedell-Avers et al., 2009; Gioia & Chittipeddi, 1991; Maitlis & Lawrence, 2007), and it is of note that for equifinality to occur, uncertainty and ambiguity characterizing an open system are necessary (Katz & Kahn, 1978). Aspects of a prescriptive mental model include *time frame orientation, type of experience used, nature of outcomes sought, number of outcomes sought, focus on model construction, locus of causation, general controllability of causation, crisis conditions, use of emotions,* and *targets of influence.* See Table 1 for a summary of the key differentiating Dimensions of CIP leaders' mental models (see Allen et al., 2020; Hunter et al., 2011 for thorough explanations of each dimension).

Table 1 Summary of the dimensions of the CIP model of leadership

Dimension	Definition
1. Time frame orientation	• The temporal reference point used to steer the construction of a prescriptive mental model, guiding the selection and organization of key causes and goals (i.e., future, present, or the past)
2. Type of experience used	• The use of positive or negative examples to influence the construction of mental models (i.e., positive examples of successful change, failure of the current system, or combination)
3. Nature of outcomes sought	• The type of goals or outcomes highlighted to frame mental model construction (i.e., positive, transcendent, or malleable)
4. Number of outcomes sought	• The focus on a number of goals or outcomes in accordance with a prescriptive mental model (i.e., multiple, selected few, or variable)
5. Focus on model construction	• The orientation toward internal or external demands as a guide to the construction of a prescriptive mental model (i.e., internal vs. external)
6. Locus of causation	• The beliefs that govern how one sees the key causal forces that should be considered in the construction of a prescriptive mental model (i.e., people, the situation, or an interaction)
7. Controllability of causation	• The beliefs one holds about an individual's ability to control the emphasized locus of causation (i.e., high, low, or variable)

Table 1 (cont.)

Dimension	Definition
8. Targets of influence	• The follower(s) that a leader intends to direct their message or appeal toward (i.e., mass groups, those with similar beliefs, or select elites)
9. Crisis conditions	• The contexts in which leader differences are most likely to emerge (i.e., ordered, chaotic, or localized)
10. Use of emotions	• The use (or lack) of emotion as an influence tactic to communicate important information to followers to motivate action (i.e., positive, negative, or rational)

This work on leader experiences reveals that individuals are unlikely to experience events that position them solely into one specific leader orientation. Instead, it is probable that key life events will result in some combination of experiences that provide foundational elements that lead to the development of various leader orientations (three of which we present in our model). Thus, although a *primary* style may exist for a given leader, by taking a profile perspective, mixed orientations are likely more prevalent than early work on historical leaders might have specified (Hunter & Lovelace, 2020). To facilitate a discussion of how leaders may (or may not) navigate their mixed-orientation profile, it is important to first acknowledge the existence of this more nuanced approach to understanding a leader's baseline mental model.

1.3.3 Navigating Mixed Orientations

Acknowledging the existence of mixed-leader-orientation profiles raises several questions: How do leaders navigate between different aspects of their profiles to utilize different leadership pathways? Can all leaders navigate between different profiles? Are the most successful leaders those that can adopt different types of orientations to utilize varying leadership pathways? Before detailing the key variables that dictate a leader's ability to utilize multiple pathways successfully, we want to make it clear that at this point, we are not arguing that the most effective leaders are those that navigate between various pathways. Instead, we are simply highlighting that leaders have the potential to possess characteristics of various recognized leader orientations as a part of a broader orientation profile. We come back to the discussion of leader effectiveness after outlining our proposed process model of leadership.

To navigate between the use of mixed-orientation profiles in the sensemaking process, leaders must demonstrate two characteristics. First, based on our previous discussion of crucible life and leadership experiences, a leader must have the prerequisite previous experiences essential to the development of different leader orientations. Without these experiences, the leader will not have developed the appropriate mental model framework mechanisms to facilitate the sensemaking process via alternative orientation pathways. These key experiences create the cognitive "tool kit" for leaders – they offer the lenses in their worldview glasses – that can enable them to use these various leadership pathways. Essentially, it is not possible for the leader to take the perspective of a given orientation without the proper frame of reference.

More centrally, to engage in multiple pathways, a leader must possess a critical cognitive ability that enables them to alternate between various pathways. Namely, high levels of cognitive complexity (Suedfelt & Tetlock, 2014), or a leader's process of thinking in a multidimensional and nuanced manner, is a key moderator of whether leaders will be able to effectively utilize multiple pathways. Taking a profile approach, Hunter and Lovelace (2020) argue that each leader orientation is not mutually exclusive. However, stark differences can be drawn that demonstrate the disparate components of each path. Thus, apart from possessing characteristics of the orientation, to switch and reconcile the differences between pathways, leaders must hold the ability to process and think in a multiplex and nuanced fashion (i.e., high cognitive complexity). Leaders high on cognitive complexity have a higher tolerance for ambiguity, can consider alternative views, and show greater strategic flexibility (Nadkarni & Naryanan, 2007; Streufert et al., 1968). Essentially, individuals high in cognitive complexity demonstrate greater mental flexibility as they have the ability to use more categories of mental schemas to process complex situational stimuli (Hooijberg et al., 1997). High cognitive complexity enables leaders to change their mental approach to a given situation, changing the way they process information, make decisions, and take action (Boal & Hooijberg, 2000; Porac & Thomas, 2002). As such, the ability to think in cognitively complex ways and fully appreciate the range of tools at a leader's disposal will serve as necessary preconditions that allow leaders to engage in a blended pathway approach and alternate between pathways should they see such variability as useful.

1.4 The Influence of a Leader's Orientation on Follower Motivation and Effort

Addressing several criticisms of modern leadership theory (e.g., see Van Knippenberg & Sitkin, 2013), Hunter and Lovelace (2020) transitioned from discussing how a leaders' worldview is formed to how followers respond to these unique leadership approaches. Specifically, it appears that differing approaches are associated with motivational and effort mechanisms on the part of the follower. To be clear, the focus is on the *unique* mechanisms that are associated with each of the three primary styles, and as such, we describe the distinctive aspects that differentiate each style rather than those that are common among all approaches to leading. Followers who like a leader personally due to qualities such as charisma, similarity, and attractiveness or view that leader as technically competent in their roles will likely garner greater commitment and broad motivational appeal regardless of what pathway is taken (e.g., DeRue et al., 2011). Again, we will focus later in the Element on those mechanisms unique to each pathway before introducing how follower expectancy mechanisms will influence the described relationships.

1.4.1 Charismatic Leadership: How Followers Respond

The charismatic pathway is associated with the utilization of a compelling, future, and change-oriented vision that is laden with positive affect and the promise of better things to come *if* the leader, and their associated vision, is followed (Hunter et al., 2011; Mumford, 2006). As such, subordinates who are convinced that a charismatic pathway leads to outcomes of value will respond to leader behaviors with similar positivity, affect, and emotion. The result is increased energy and engagement on work tasks.

A charismatic pathway is linked with greater energy and effort, in part, due to the emotional contagion effect whereby followers automatically transfer emotions from the leader or "catch" the emotions and respond similarly as a result (Bono & Ilies, 2006; Johnson, 2008). Thus, we predict that leaders who are engaging the development of a positively charged, compelling vision will pass along that positivity to their followers via automatic or unconscious processes. Indeed, George (2000) found that leaders exhibiting positive affect produced similar levels of positive affect in their subordinates. Bono and Ilies (2006), similarly, found that when leaders were rated as being inspirational and using behaviors associated with idealized influence, they evoked more positive affect and that effect was linked to positive mood states of followers. In light of such findings and others (e.g., Bono et al., 2007), it seems reasonable to argue that followers experience a greater amount of positive emotion when interacting with a leader utilizing a change-oriented leadership approach.

Critically, positive affect has been shown to be a key predictor of several organizational outcomes, including engagement, defined as "a relatively enduring state of mind referring to the simultaneous investment of personal energies in the experience or performance of work" (Christian et al., 2011, p. 95). In their meta-analysis of the work engagement literature, for example, Christian and colleagues (2011) found that positive affect was the strongest predictor of work engagement, producing effect sizes that rivaled important job-related attributes such as autonomy, task variety, task significance, and feedback. Moreover, there is the potential for a compounding, spiraling effect whereby increased engagement may increase positive affect leading to growing levels of engagement as well as increased social connections that further enhance engagement (Bakker et al., 2014; Fredrickson, 2001).

Further evidence for increased effort on the part of followers may be seen, albeit indirectly, in a range of studies demonstrating links between vision-based efforts and increased engagement and performance (e.g., Judge et al., 2004; Lowe et al., 1996). In a recent study, for example, Babcock-Roberson and Strickland (2010) found that leader charismatic behaviors, which are aligned with a change-oriented approach, were associated with greater follower engagement. Finally, there has been an indication that vision-based approaches to leadership can result in so much increased effort that it may be harmful to followers if high levels of emotional engagement are sustained over a long period (Yukl, 1999). The implication here is that the change-oriented pathway is one characterized by high energy, positive emotion, and high effort and engagement on the part of the follower and, in some cases, extremely so.

1.4.2 Ideological Leadership: How Followers Respond

In contrast to a charismatic approach, an ideological approach is characterized by a connection over a shared set of beliefs, with the leader offering to improve followers' lives by ushering in a return to key values that are perceived by the follower as having been lost or relegated (Lovelace et al., 2019; Mumford, 2006). Recall from earlier equifinality models that ideological leaders frequently utilize negative emotion and warn of harmful outcomes if their pathway is not chosen. As such, we propose that followers drawn to an ideological leader will respond with greater compliance due to the fear of harmful outcomes as well as be willing to sacrifice due to a strong commitment to the leader and the core values they represent.

As with the change-oriented style, we also predict an emotional contagion effect whereby leaders will promote negative emotion such as fear and anxiety, resulting in felt emotion on the part of the follower. Rather than experiencing greater engagement, however, we argue that this approach results in greater deference and willingness to concede to the leader. This submissive phenomenon is known as the centralization-of-authority thesis (e.g., Helmreich, 1979; Janis, 1954). The premise is that deference to a leader is given because a leader best represents the core values of the organization and is in the best position to make decisions that are suitable for the larger collective. Thus, to the extent that a leader successfully promotes fear and enumerates external sources of stress to garner support, so too will obedience to that leader increase.

This proposed deference mechanism is inherently linked to how strongly a leader is seen to embody a subordinate's beliefs and values. That is, a leader must be perceived as being representative of what a subordinate holds most dear for that leader to receive greater authority during times of fear, anxiety, and stress. This premise also fits under the umbrella of an emerging social identity perspective, whereby obedience to a leader is predicated on a leader being seen as the embodiment of a follower's values. Haslam and colleagues (2015) use the term "engaged followership" to describe this phenomenon and have begun reanalyzing early seminal work by Milgram (1963), proposing that participants engaged in continued harm (i.e., shocking via a device) of study confederates not simply due to blind deference to authority but because the experimenter was the personification of what they valued. As Haslam and colleagues note, "Indeed, they continued shocking precisely because these consequences were ones they supported and identified with, and because their actions were construed to be contributing to a moral, worthy, and progressive cause" (p. 6). Thus, leaders who utilize an ideological pathway via the promotion of fear and anxiety, while simultaneously indicating that they characterize the values and beliefs of subordinates, will have at their disposal loyal subordinates who are willing to defer to them as near singular sources of guidance and direction. By extension, should they be asked to do so, followers on the ideological path are more willing to undergo personal sacrifice on the part of the leader.

1.4.3 Pragmatic Leadership: How Followers Respond

Leaders utilizing a pragmatic approach seek to provide advancement and progress through cogent problem-solving (Mumford, 2006). Those with a pragmatic orientation focus on being rational, informed, and measured in their leadership. Emotion, on the positive or negative ends of the affect spectrum, is utilized less often, and leaders taking the pragmatic path focus on localized and present state issues as a means to make longer-term progress (Hunter et al., 2011). As such, followers drawn to leaders utilizing more pragmatic tactics do not engage in raucously enthusiastic work behaviors or operate as deferential followers eagerly willing to sacrifice for the cause, but rather have a clear sense of purpose and, more importantly, clarity about *how* to proceed. Leaders utilizing a pragmatic style make it evident what behaviors are required to solve a given problem or meet a specified goal, and as such, followers are more efficient in their work roles.

Given the focus on clarity and efficiency as the effort mechanism for followers in the pragmatic approach, it is worth noting expressly that the effectiveness of the style is not directly linked to motivation per se. Instead, leaders utilizing this approach succeed because they make efficient use of their resources and subordinate talents, in particular. Although emotion can be a powerful motivating mechanism, there are downsides (Yukl, 1999). An example such as downside is the potential for wasted effort. That is, when when influenced by other leadership styles (e.g., charismatic) followers may operate in a more frenetic and emotionally charged fashion. The pragmatic approach, in contrast, succeeds due to its lack of wasted resources and an emphasis on proficiency in problem-solving. Thus,

in sum, the three proposed styles are focused on primarily influencing distinct forms of motivation and effort. Followers that respond to the charismatic pathway will experience greater energy, enthusiasm, and engagement. Those influenced by the ideological style will defer to the leader, being more obedient and willing to sacrifice if asked by the leader to do so. Finally, followers who respond to a pragmatic approach are not inherently more motivated by their personal connection to the leader but are committed to solving the problems clearly defined by the leader, operating in a coolly efficient manner. As such, the CIP theory explains three leader orientations that guide motivation and effort pathways associated with follower and organizational success (i.e., an equifinality approach).

1.5 Personalized and Socialized Leadership: A Branch on the Pathways

The CIP theory of leadership is, in a sense, agnostic about the utilization and application of influence. That is, the framework makes no specific predictions about whether leaders will use their influence for good or ill (Mumford et al., 2020). Consider the following contrasting approaches to leadership within the same core pathway. Betty Freidan, leader in the feminist movement who advocated for equal rights, was an ideological leader, as was Pol Pot, head of Cambodia's communist movement whose policies led to the horrific deaths of 1.8 million Cambodians. Margaret Thatcher was a charismatic leader who served as the first female prime minister of England and led Britain through the Falklands War giving British citizens a renewed sense of pride and patriotism, as was Herman Goering, president of the Reichstag in Nazi Germany who helped contribute to the atrocities of World War II. Alfred du Pont was a pragmatic leader whose successful businesses continue to support charities today, as was Al Capone, a mob boss in Chicago whose organization murdered countless individuals while engaging in illegal activities (Mumford, 2006).

These contrasting examples of leaders help illustrate that within the categories of the CIP, there is substantial variability in how each pathway of influence is applied.

In his original framing of the theory, Mumford (2006) utilized the work of House and Howell (1992) to provide guidance as to when and why some leaders engaged in more destructive acts and others worked for the good of their fellow humans. More superficially, Mumford placed 120 leaders into the categories of charismatic, ideological, or pragmatic as well as the two power orientation categories of personalized or socialized. According to House and Howell (1992), Mumford (2006), and Watts and colleagues (2018), personalized leaders utilize influence to benefit themselves or for personal gain. In contrast, socialized leaders utilize their influence to benefit collective goals or for the greater good. This distinction between personalized and socialized orientation adds a critical layer of understanding to the CIP theory. That is, the CIP theory helps explain how influence is garnered from followers, and the personalized/socialized distinction helps explain how that influence is used by the leader.

2 Methods: How the CIP Theory Has Been Studied

2.1 Historiometric Foundations

To understand the origins of the CIP theory, it is useful to understand the methods used to study it. The most prominent method during the development of the theory was historiometric (Crayne & Hunter, 2018; Ligon et al., 2012). The historiometric method represents an approach of study that allows for quantitative analysis of qualitative data. The most common historiometric study uses academic biographies and trained coders to measure constructs that are chosen and operationalized before coding begins. The method is labor-intensive and time-consuming, requiring significant effort to acquire and vet the source material even before the arduous process of coding and aggregation begins. One significant advantage of such an approach, however, is intimacy and rich connection with what is being studied. That is, each quantitative value or data point that is derived from the method is the result of a long string of curated tasks, each requiring attention, focus, and judgment from a human coder or biographer. Along related lines, once values are derived from the coding process and trends observed when analyzing data, it is possible for the researcher to go back to the original source material and make sense of findings in a way not possible using more traditional survey methods most commonly applied in leadership research (Hunter et al., 2007).

One reason it is critical to understand the role historiometric analysis has played in the development of the CIP theory is that if more traditional methods had been utilized, the theory is not likely to have emerged. That is, the novel historiometric method allowed for the development of the novel CIP theoretical framework that stands in contrast to many established theories of leadership. Specifically, using content analysis of qualitative data allows for the investigation of leadership styles such as pragmatic leadership that would not emerge in a study using methods such as surveys or self-reports. In a recent review of the methods utilized in CIP studies, Watts and colleagues (2020) found that the majority of CIP empirical studies utilized relied on historiometric approaches (57%). While some studies examined specific CIP styles in isolation, the overwhelming majority (75%) examined all three in combination. While the historiometric approach helped establish a strong foundation for CIP theory, future advancement of the research stream will require additional creative approaches (Antonakis & Day, 2018).

The historiometric approach, although advantageous for many reasons, is not without its flaws. Previously mentioned is the time-consuming and labor-intensive nature of the methodological approach. In addition, the historiometric method requires that a leader have information compiled and developed on them (e.g., a biography). This means that the approach is typically only applied to high-level leaders who are likely to have received such attention, and issues of generalizability emerge when considering other types of leaders that do not receive such widespread recognition. That is, a reasonable question can be asked as to whether what is learned by studying world leaders and CEOs can be applied to more typical forms of leadership. In response to such criticisms, other researchers have begun to utilize methods such as experimental as well as the development of new scales in efforts to expand the population of leaders considered by CIP research. Watts and colleagues (2020) outline the emerging methodological approaches in the CIP research stream and observe that although historiometric approaches were used initially, experimental approaches have become more commonplace (Thoroughgood & Sawyer, 2017; Tsai, 2017). They found that 32 percent of CIP studies have used experimental methods, expanding the methodological pool of CIP research. Still, one issue hampering the expansion of samples and broader investigation has been that of measurement. Limited psychometric tools (e.g., easy to administer and time-friendly scales) currently prevent CIP researchers from studying leaders in more applied settings. However, recent efforts suggest that scaling and measuring CIP is possible using a new measure.

2.2 Experimental Efforts

While the majority of CIP studies rely on historiometric or case-study-based approaches, there are also a growing number of experimental efforts that examine the CIP model of leadership. The majority of these CIP experimental efforts focus on the outcomes associated with exposure to leaders demonstrating the various CIP leadership styles. For example, Kotlyar and colleagues (2011) and Lovelace and Hunter (2013) trained confederates (i.e., actors) to display characteristics of CIP leaders based on differences in their mental models. Kotlyar and colleagues (2011) examined the effects of charismatic and pragmatic leaders on follower team commitment and problem-solving. Meanwhile, Lovelace and Hunter (2013) studied the impact of CIP leadership styles on follower creative performance across the different stages of the problem-solving process. Other studies used written descriptions or verbal examples of different CIP leaders to examine follower leadership style preferences (Thoroughgood & Swayer, 2017), ethical decision-making (Watts et al., 2018), or creative performance (Griffith et al., 2018). Whether simulating CIP styles in lab settings with actors fulfilling the role of the leader or exposing study participants to written or verbal examples of actual CIP leader communication, these experimental approaches have helped expand our knowledge about the outcomes associated with the various CIP leadership styles, building the credibility of the equifinality perspective of leadership.

That said, experimental efforts focused on examining the CIP model of leadership from the perspective of the leader have been limited. As an exception, Bedell-Avers and colleagues (2008) and Hunter and colleagues (2009) both categorized college student participants into charismatic, ideological, or pragmatic styles by having the participants read several stories about CIP leaders and indicate which leader was most similar to them. Following established methods (Mumford et al., 2002), the participants were categorized as charismatic, ideological, or pragmatic leaders based on their preferences for the leaders in the presented story excerpts. After classifying the leaders based on style, the studies then asked the participants to solve complex leadership problems, providing insight into how situational factors influence the impact of the individuals' charismatic, ideological, or pragmatic style on performance.

The expansion of the use of experimental studies in CIP research facilitates the ability of the research to impose control measures that allow researchers to draw stronger causal inferences about research findings overall. However, these experimental approaches are not without limitations. The use of trained actors or paper people studies raises concerns about the generalizability of the findings to actual leaders in real-world settings (Watts et al., 2020). Second, while the efforts of Bedell and colleagues (2008) do a good job identifying individuals' CIP style, the method utilized is time- and resource-intensive, making the wide-scale examination of current leaders in real-world situations difficult. As a result, CIP research has seen limited progress in expanding beyond its historiometric origins. Efforts to expand the measures and methods available to investigate the CIP leaders in current organizations will help broaden the number of opportunities to contribute to the research stream.

2.3 Emerging Methods

With the limitations of previous CIP research in mind, recent efforts aimed to expand the methodological tool kit of CIP research moving forward. For example, Lovelace and colleagues (2020) introduced a new CIP model of a leadership scale. The CIP scale effort aimed to provide a measure that can be used in both lab and field research. Drawing from previous CIP research, Lovelace and colleagues (2020) conceptually combined some of the CIP mental model dimensions that overlap significantly and put an emphasis on examining the dimensions that demonstrate the most differentiation (e.g., Bedell-Avers et al., 2008; Hunter et al., 2009). Drawing from Hunter and colleagues (2011), Lovelace and colleagues' (2020, p. 84) measure focused on four CIP mental model dimensions: (1) *leader identity* (i.e., how an individual sees themselves and their role in relation to others in the organization), (2) *nature of goals sought* (i.e., the types of outcomes that a leader emphasizes as the desired end state*)*, (3) *targets of influence* (i.e., the type of follower that the leader sees as essential to gain influence and support from to achieve an end state), and (4) *nature of appeals* (i.e., how the leader affectively/rationally frames the situation and their message). See Table 2 for a summary of these key differentiating dimensions.

In their scale development effort, Lovelace and colleagues built a CIP scale based on the conceptual foundation originally presented by Mumford (2006) in hopes of expanding future opportunities for CIP research. Utilizing a variety of student and working participant samples, they confirmed and replicated a hierarchical (two-level) factor scale structure for a thirty-six-item measure that captures the four mental model dimensions for each CIP leadership style. Instead of assigning people to one specific CIP leadership style, the scale measures ratings for all three styles. Lovelace and colleagues (2020) argue that this approach will facilitate future investigation of mixed-model CIP styles (i.e., leadership styles that exhibit characteristics of multiple CIP leadership styles). The scale development effort established initial construct validity evidence based on results showing a number of predicted relationships with other established leadership measures. Finally, the scale effort identified initial

Table 2 Key differentiating dimensions from Lovelace and colleagues (2020) CIP scale development

1. Leader identity	Summarizes how an individual sees their role in relation to others in the organization	C – bring positive Future I – values bearer P – problem solver
2. Nature of goals sought	Identifies types of outcomes the leader emphasizes as the desired end state	C – broad perspective I – values focused P – specific to problems
3. Targets of influence	Addresses the type of follower that the leader sees as essential to influence to achieve the desired end state	C – mass groups I – shared beliefs P – specific experts
4. Nature of appeals	Describes the way a leader affectively or rationally frames the situation and their message to influence others	C – positive focus I – negative appeal P – rational appeal

criterion validity support based on its ability to predict the quality of leader performance on two problem-solving tasks with results that account for variance beyond current leadership scales. To further investigate the utility of the CIP scale and to examine CIP theory's applicability to an applied sample of current leaders, Lascano and colleagues (2020) explored the distribution of CIP styles in a global sample of applied leaders and examined the relationship of leadership style to a variety of employee engagement outcomes. Broadly, their results indicate that many leaders in global organizations have distinct leadership styles but that these styles are also related to organizational outcomes. The effort of Lascano and colleagues (2020) provides additional evidence for the utility of the CIP scale while also raising important questions for CIP research to consider moving forward.

3 CIP Leadership Research Findings: What Researchers Have Discovered

With an understanding of how CIP research has been conducted, we now turn our attention to the major themes that have emerged from the CIP research stream. Mumford's (2006) examination of 120 historical leader biographies laid a critical foundation of support for the CIP theory. Through several studies examining different aspects of the CIP model of leadership, this Element created a strong foundational and comprehensive understanding of the similarities and differences between CIP leaders. This collection of studies also established key areas of study for the CIP stream of research, including the emergence and development of CIP leaders (e.g., Mumford et al., 2006b, 2006f), the influence of leaders on performance (Mumford et al., 2006g), the important differences in leader's approaches to problem-solving (Mumford et al., 2006a), the relationship between different leadership styles and interactions with followers (Mumford et al., 2006h), and differences in the influence mechanisms used by leaders with different styles (Mumford et al., 2006c, 2006d). As a baseline, these studies found support for the basic premise of the CIP theory that there are multiple pathways to achieving effective leadership.

In more than fifteen years since the release of Mumford (2006), the research stream has received consistent attention, and our understanding of the CIP model of leadership continues to grow as a result. In particular, inspired by the themes of the various studies in Mumford (2006), several areas of research have expanded; for example, studies on the impact of CIP leadership styles on problem-solving (Bedell-Avers et al., 2008; Lovelace & Hunter, 2013), influence tactics (Griffith et al., 2015; Hunter et al., 2011), and follower interactions (Griffith et al., 2015; Thoroughgood & Sawyer, 2017) have all added strong support for the guiding principles of the CIP theory. See Table 3 for a summary of all CIP research findings. Later in the Element, we synthesize some of the major findings and themes from the rich history of the CIP model of leadership research stream.

3.1 Leader Mental Model Differences

As previously described, the foundational differences between CIP leaders stem from the differences in their cognitive orientations (i.e., their individual mental models; Allen et al., 2020; Lovelace et al., 2019). Differences in the mental models of leaders determine how leaders go about their sensemaking processes; in other words, how leaders identify, interpret, and react to various situations (e.g., Mumford, 2006). Basically, a leader's sensemaking process determines how they make decisions about their organization's response to complex problems, which has important implications for individuals and organizational outcomes with significant ramifications for various individual and firm outcomes (e.g., Gioia & Chittipeddi, 1991; Maitlis & Christianson, 2014).

Again, the work of Mumford and colleagues has identified several dimensions that differentiate the mental models of the CIP leadership styles: *time frame orientation, type of experience used, nature of outcomes sought, number of outcomes sought, focus on model construction, locus of causation,* and *general controllability of causation, crisis conditions, use of emotions,* and

Table 3a Summary of Findings on Leader Mental Model & Problem-Solving Differences in the CIP Research Literature

Theme	Citation	Method	Main Contributions
Leader Mental Models Differences	Mumford & Van Doorn (2001)	Case Study	• Defines pragmatic leadership as appeal to interests instead of identity, identifying focus on current problems and commitment to logical appeals/ rational persuasion
	Hunter, Cushenbery, Thoroughgood, Johnson, & Ligon (2011)	Empirical - Historiometric	• Establishes broad support for CIP differentiating mental model factor dimensionality in college and NFL football coaches
	Mumford, Gaddis, Licuanan, Ersland, & Siekel (2006)	Empirical - Historiometric	• Multiple significant interactions between CIP leader style and socialized vs personalized orientation
	Mumford, Strange, Gaddis, Licuanan & Scott (2006)	Empirical - Historiometric	• Multiple interactive effects between CIP Style and socialized vs personalized orientation on various outcomes of interest.
	Bedell-Avers, Hunter, Angie, Eubanks, Mumford (2009)	Case Study	• Identifies the impact of a leader's prescriptive mental model on their interaction with other leaders • Distinguishes how CIP leaders work together, and if they can work together

	Watts, Steele, & Mumford (2018)	Empirical - Experimental	• Demonstrates the importance of charismatic and pragmatic story-telling in understanding the influence of leader mental models
	Lovelace, Hunter, & Neely (2020)	Empirical - Experimental	• Establishes initial evidence for a CIP model of leadership psychometric scale
Problem-Solving Approach	Mumford, Strange, Gaddis, Licuanan & Scott (2006)	Empirical - Historiometric	• While CIP leaders don't differ in their general contributions to society, they do differ in how they contribute.
	Mumford, Bedell, Hunter, Espejo, & Boatman (2006)	Empirical - Historiometric	• CIP leaders produce problem solutions of varying quality during their rise to power vs the pinnacle of their power • Leaders focus on different elements of the problem-solving process to address challenges
Leader Developmental Experience Differences	Mumford, Scott, Marcy, Tutt, & Espejo (2006)	Empirical - Historiometric	• Leader's frequency of specific types of critical life events relates to their CIP style later in life
	Ligon, Hunter, & Mumford (2008)	Empirical - Historiometric	• CIP leaders differ in the number of redemption, anchoring, turning point, and originating events experienced in development
	Mumford, Bedell, & Scott (2006)	Empirical - Historiometric	• CIP leaders' differing critical development experiences relate to specific leader behaviors and key outcomes

Table 3b Summary of Key Findings on Leader Interpersonal Differences in the CIP Research Literature

Theme	Citation	Method	Main Contributions
Influence Mechanisms	Strange & Mumford (2002)	Empirical - Historiometric	• Ideological leaders demonstrate greater focus on value autonomy and value commitment than charismatic leaders • Charismatic and ideological leaders are both likely to display vision-based leadership behaviors
	Mumford, Licuanan, Marcy, Dailey, & Blair (2006)	Empirical - Historiometric	• CIP leader styles more likely to use certain influence tactics (pragmatic - expertise and control of resources; charismatic - status perceptions; charismatic and ideological - coalition building)
	Mumford, Espejo, Hunter, Bedell-Avers, Eubanks, & Connelly (2007)	Empirical - Historiometric	• Ideological leaders are more prone to violence than charismatic leaders and differ in terms of their just-world commitments, ideological extremism, oppositional bonding, imposition of interpretive structures, value-based control, and social disruption

	Griffith, Connelly, Theil, & Johnson (2015)	Empirical - Historiometric	• Charismatic leaders display more use of positive emotions; ideological leaders display more use of negative emotions; pragmatic leaders use more rational persuasion • Charismatic leaders use more soft influence tactics and ideological leaders use more hard influence tactics
Leader-Follower Interactions & Relationships	Mumford, Strange, Scott, Dailey, & Blair (2006)	Empirical - Historiometric	• Ideological leaders have close relationships with followers, providing followers the opportunity to exercise influence and significant autonomy • Charismatic leaders tend to have higher ratings of mutual exchange support with followers than ideological and pragmatic leaders (ideological leaders > pragmatic leaders)
	Kotlyar, Karakowsky, & Ng (2011)	Empirical - Experimental	• Pragmatic leader most effective at encouraging member commitment to team generated decisions, based on restraining dysfunctional conflict
	Griffith, Connelly, Theil, & Johnson (2015)	Empirical - Historiometric	• Pragmatic leaders are perceived to be more emotionally authentic • Ideological leaders are perceived to be more emotionally volatile

Table 3b (cont.)

Theme	Citation	Method	Main Contributions
	Thoroughgood & Sawyer (2017)	Empirical - Vignette	• By using a follower-centric lens, identifies for whom CIP leaders are most appealing and influential • Categorizes two follower individual difference profiles, personality function and work values function, which impact follower CIP leader preferences
	Griffith, Gibson, Medeiros, MacDougall, Hardy, & Mumford (2018)	Empirical – Lab Study	• CIP leader style and leader distance interact to shape follower creative outcomes • While general mental model congruence is not predictive of follower performance, alignment on types of experience, nature of outcomes and use of emotions were most important dimensions of mental model congruence

Table 3c Summary of Findings on the Importance of Situational Factors in the CIP Research Literature

Theme	Citation	Method	Main Contributions
Cultural and Demographic Differences	Lascano, Boatman, Strange, & Walters (2020)	Empirical – Applied survey sample	• Pragmatic leader styles are most common, followed by charismatic and finally ideological. • There are some cultural differences in the emergence of leader styles (i.e., pattern is not uniform across cultures) although the general observation that most leaders are pragmatic, followed by charismatic, and ideological is consistent • There is some indication that women are more likely to engage in a pragmatic style (although work remains here)
The Influence of Context on CIP leadership	Mumford, Antes, Caughron, & Friedrich (2008)	Theory	• Identifies various multi-level conditions that impact the emergence and performance of CIP leaders at the individual, group, organizational, and broader environmental level
	Bedell-Avers, Hunter, Mumford (2008)	Empirical – Lab Study	• Specific contextual conditions better facilitate the performance of certain CIP leader styles in specific situations, but not across conditions • Charismatic leaders performed best on problems that allowed for flexibility, ideological leaders excelled when identified as the leader, and

Table 3c (cont.)

Theme	Citation	Method	Main Contributions
			pragmatic leaders were consistent across contextual conditions
	Hunter, Bedell-Avers, & Mumford (2009)	Empirical – Lab Study	• Situational complexity and framing influence the success of CIP leaders in specific situations, but not across conditions
			• Charismatic leaders excelled except in highly complex situations, ideological leaders struggled complex situations not aligned with their belief system, and pragmatic leaders were consistent across conditions
	Lovelace & Hunter (2013)	Empirical – Lab Study	• On short duration problem-solving tasks, charismatic and ideological leaders' followers outperformed pragmatic followers, suggesting pragmatic leaders need more time to emerge
			• Charismatic leader followers outperform ideological and pragmatic followers on idea generation task solution originality
	Crayne & Medeiros (2020)	Case Study	• Examines the differences of CIP leaders to the COVID-19 Crisis, discusses the advantages and disadvantages of each approach

targets of influence (e.g., see Table 1; Hunter et al., 2011; Mumford et al., 2006e). Together, these factors provide the lens through which leaders develop their prescriptive mental model. Early findings in CIP work aimed to examine the differences between leaders on these foundational mental model differences. In particular, the studies included in Mumford (2006) developed strong initial support for dimensional variations in leaders' mental models (e.g., Hunter et al., 2011; Mumford et al., 2006e, 2006g). The key findings from these studies connect differences in these mental model dimensions and leader decisions and behaviors in organizations (e.g., Griffith et al., 2015; Mumford et al., 2006h, 2007; Strange & Mumford, 2005).

3.2 Leader Problem-Solving

One key area of research on differences in leader actions center on how variations in mental models influence a leader's approach solving problems. Ultimately, a key requirement of fulfilling the leadership role is addressing difficult problems in organizations, and understanding differences in CIP leaders problem-solving approaches illuminates how these different leadership styles achieve success through different approaches (Bedell-Avers et al., 2009; Hunter et al., 2009; Mumford, 2006). CIP leaders' mental model differences lead them to focus on the use of different skills or processes when they attempt to understand and address problem-solving (Mumford, 2002; Mumford & Van Doorn, 2001; Mumford et al., 2006b). Difficult or uncertain situations require fewer clear-cut solutions, and as a result, differences in leadership approaches become much more likely to emerge based on the discretion leaders have when making decisions (Lubart, 2001; Mumford, 2006).

For example, several CIP studies have identified differences in leader problem-solving at specific stages of the overall problem-solving process (Hunter et al., 2011; Mumford et al., 1991). There are three main stages to the problem-solving process, each with several substages: early stage (problem identification, information gathering, and concept selection), middle stage (conceptual combination and idea generation), and late stage (idea evaluation, implementation planning, and monitoring; Lovelace et al., 2017). CIP research shows that charismatic leaders focus on the use of positive goals, and the key role of people in helping solve problems leads them to emphasize idea generation, an essential substage of the middle stage of the problem-solving (Mumford et al., 2004, 2006a). The focus on the importance of past success leads ideological leaders to emphasize evaluative activities critical to the late stages of problem-solving that relate to the implementation of successful plans (Lovelace et al., 2017; Mumford et al., 2006a). Finally, as pragmatic leaders focus on current issues and the importance of logic, they tend to emphasize clearly defining key elements of a problem, an important part of the early stages of problem-solving (Mumford, 2006; Mumford & Van Doorn, 2001). While CIP research does not identify overall differences in problem-solving success, evidence supports the idea that CIP leaders effectively navigate the overall problem-solving process by focusing on different stages of the overall process (Lovelace et al., 2019).

3.3 Origins of CIP Leader Mental Models and Life Experience

After developing support for the differences in leader mental models and sensemaking approaches, the CIP research sought to understand how these differences develop. Mumford and colleagues (2006f) argued from a conceptual standpoint that these differences originate from key experiences during a leader's individual development (Ligon et al., 2008; Mumford et al., 2006e). In particular, key developmental experiences play an important role in constructing an individual's identity, establishing values systems, and shaping how leaders work to achieve goals and shape the interpretation of current events based on these key past experiences (McAdams, 2006; Mobley et al., 1992; Mumford et al., 2006e; Pillemer, 2001).

As mentioned previously in our discussion, when examining the importance of key life experiences of CIP leadership, Ligon and colleagues (2008) found that charismatic, ideological, and pragmatic leaders differed in terms of the frequency of which they were exposed to certain types of key life events. Specifically, the researchers found that charismatic leaders were more likely to have experienced a greater number of *turning point events*. These events prepare a leader for dealing with uncertainty as they force an individual to deal with a critical event redirecting life's direction, resulting in changes to an individual's objectives or motivations in life. Ideological leaders were more likely to experience more *anchoring events*, which are events that reinforce the importance of maintaining key values and beliefs. Finally, pragmatic leaders were more likely to be exposed to a greater number of *originating events* that emphasize the importance of incremental progress and the importance of using facts and logic when solving problems. So far, the evidence suggests that key life experiences are important to the development of the mental models and sensemaking activities of CIP leaders. Furthermore, they play an important role in determining how leaders view, understand, and act on information in organizations (Strange & Mumford, 2002, 2005).

3.4 CIP Leader Communication Approaches

Because many of the differences between CIP leaders are cognitive in nature, a good portion of CIP research examines how these mental models emerge in a leader's efforts to communicate with and influence others (Griffith et al., 2015; Mumford et al., 2006e). Based on the differences in their mental models, CIP leaders' approaches to communicating with and influencing others differ significantly in a variety of ways (Mumford et al., 2006b; Strange & Mumford, 2002). First, while charismatic and ideological leaders both used vision-based appeals to attract and influence followers, the content of their messages differ quite a bit (Strange & Mumford, 2002). Strange and Mumford identified that while ideological leaders, versus charismatic leaders, put greater emphasis on the importance of adherence to certain key values or beliefs to accomplish their organizational vision. Additionally, Mumford and colleagues (2006b) found that charismatic leaders influenced others by promoting status perceptions and the attractiveness of the future success associated with the implementation of their vision. Next, charismatic and ideological leaders aimed to build broader bases of support from groups of people than pragmatic leaders. Finally, pragmatic leaders were more likely to exert influence through expertise (i.e., through reasoning, rationality, personal knowledge) and through resource control than charismatic or ideological leaders. While leaders regardless of their CIP style aimed to address complex problems in organizations, the specific influence tactics they used to support the implementation of their vision or plan differed.

A growing number of studies identify the emotional displays of CIP leaders as another key area that behavior differences manifest (i.e., Griffith et al., 2015; Mumford et al., 2006c). Not only do leader emotional displays (or reliance on less emotional rational displays) help differentiate CIP leadership styles, but a number of studies have connected these differences to key outcomes for followers and organizations (Griffith et al., 2015; Mumford & Van Doorn, 2001; Strange & Mumford, 2002). Hunter and colleagues (2011) examined how college and NFL coaches demonstrated differences in various characteristics of CIP leaders in an in-depth historiometric study. They found that charismatic leaders relied more heavily on positive emotional appeals, ideological leaders used more negative emotional appeals, and pragmatic leaders used a greater number of rational or logic appeals when trying to influence others. Griffith and colleagues (2015) also found that charismatic leaders were more likely to use positive emotional appeals that relied on personal power, ideological leaders' negative emotional appeals that leveraged positional power, and pragmatic leaders focused on rational appeals that used logical arguments. These tactics led pragmatic leaders to be perceived as more authentic and ideological leaders as emotionally volatile. While the research indicates that overall performance is similar, the way that CIP leaders approach their communication and influence attempts with members of the organization differ significantly.

3.5 Leader–Follower Relationships

Based on the differences in the communication styles of CIP leaders, another key area of CIP research focuses on the differences in the relationships between leaders and followers in organizations. For example, Mumford and colleagues (2006h) examined the differences in leader–member exchange (LMX) relationships based on the CIP leadership style. They found that charismatic leaders scored highest on ratings of mutual exchange support, with pragmatic leaders scoring the lowest. They also identified that ideological leaders established close relationships with like-minded followers, often empowering these followers to influence others. As another example, Thoroughgood and Sawyer (2017) examined how follower personality profiles influenced preferences for leaders with specific CIP leadership styles. More than half of the followers in their study preferred ideological or pragmatic leaders, undermining more romanticized notions about charismatic leadership being the most desired or the most effective leadership style. More specifically, followers who were concerned with rationality, autonomy, and competition preferred pragmatic leaders. Meanwhile, team-oriented, emotionally stable, future-focused, and less rational-minded followers tended to favor charismatic leaders. Finally, individuals who put a premium on traditional values showed deference toward ideological leaders. Additionally, Griffith and colleagues (2018) further explored the relationship between leaders and followers based on the influence of the congruence between leader and follower CIP mental models' congruence on follower creative performance. Their results showed that mental model congruence was related to more original follower creative outcomes. They also found that leader–follower congruence related to the mental model dimensions of (1) types of experience used, (2) nature of outcomes sought, and (3) emotional appeals were all predictive of greater follower creativity.

3.6 Demographic and Cultural Differences

Although the origins of the CIP theory are grounded in samples spanning multiple cultures, contexts, and to a lesser degree, inclusive of women (Mumford, 2006), much of this early work was based on historical accounts and historiometric data (Crayne & Hunter, 2018). As such, there has been relatively little systematic investigation of differences in leadership styles across various demographic groups as well as cultural investigations in applied or real-world samples. This gap remains an issue in the CIP research stream. However, helping contribute to closing this gap in understanding, Lascano and colleagues (2020) examined CIP scores in a sample of 306 leaders in a large multinational organization. In their sample of established, organizational leaders, the majority fell into the pragmatic category of leadership style (61%), providing indirect support for the core notion of CIP that not all effective leaders are charismatic, and it is important to consider the range of leadership pathways as they may be even more prevalent in applied settings. The researchers also found that leaders were more likely to be ideological if they were younger (under the age of forty) and more likely to be pragmatic if they were older (over the age of forty). These differences, although subtle, do suggest that there is value in tracking leader changes over time and that work is warranted examining these longitudinal changes.

Lascano and colleagues (2020) also observed differences across subsamples that included leaders in Asia, Europe, North America, and India. A few notable findings from their study include the observation that ideological leaders were more likely to produce higher scores in Asia (15.79%) when compared to Europe (7.53%) and North American (3.26%) samples. Such results are not inconsistent with findings from the GLOBE project, where such cultures favor deference to leaders based on deep value systems as well as preferring leaders who adhere to societal norms and rules (Chhokar et al., 2007). Pragmatism, moreover, was more prevalent in the North American sample (69.57%) than in the other samples (ranging from 44.74% to 58.82%). Again, such findings are commensurate with GLOBE findings, where individuals in North America preferred a focus on outcomes and cared less about following rigid rules or norms. Bedell and colleagues (2006), for example, found that pragmatic leaders were more likely to be Machiavellian, doing whatever was necessary to achieve their goals. Finally, charismatic leadership was most prevalent in India (34%) when compared across other regions (ranging from 21.74% to 28.95%) also consistent with the GLOBE trends that in India, leaders are often afforded status privileges and viewed in a reverential manner. In the aggregate, such trends suggest cultural variability and differences in preferences for leadership styles across such cultures. It is clear that work is needed before drawing strong conclusions with regard to such differences, but these early trends suggest there is value in considering these differences more closely.

Finally, data provided by Lascano and colleagues reveal that women were more likely to be categorized as pragmatic (76.3%) when compared to men (66.2%). Women were also less likely to fall into the charismatic category (18.4%) when compared to men (23.4%) with both men and women reporting the low likelihood of ideological leader classification, although women did report a slightly lower prevalence percentage of leaders (2.6% for women and 5.2% for men). A few leaders fell into the mixed categories but were very similar across the two reported genders. Again, although these findings represent only a small sample of leaders, they do provide some insight into the potential differences and similarities across gender. We might speculate, for example, that findings are consistent with the argument that women may be viewed negatively if they display emotion by engaging in either a charismatic or ideological style (Brescoll, 2016; Brescoll et al., 2018) and may be pressured into a more pragmatic leadership style as they feel it necessary to explain and justify their leadership decisions. Future research will be necessary (see also Griffith & Medeiros, 2020), but this area of investigation appears worthy of consideration.

3.7 Context Matters

Finally, another theme emerging from the CIP research focuses on understanding how contextual factors influence the impact of CIP leadership styles. Several CIP studies consider the importance of environmental factors to further our understanding of how contexts influence the overall CIP leadership process across different conditions (Bedell et al., 2008; Lovelace & Hunter, 2013; Mumford, 2006). Several studies have examined how situational complexity, rigidity, and demands influence the success of CIP leaders.

For example, research shows that charismatic leaders' performance is enhanced in flexible situations, while ideological leaders perform better in situations where leadership roles are clearly defined (Bedell-Avers et al., 2008). Meanwhile, pragmatic leaders demonstrated consistency across various conditions regardless of the situation. Additionally, Hunter and colleagues (2009) found that specific situational conditions played to the strengths of certain leadership styles. In another study, charismatic leaders had more difficulty navigating complex conditions that did not align with their future-focused vision, and ideological leaders struggled to deal with situations that did not align well with their belief system (Hunter et al., 2009). However, ideological leaders really excelled when their belief system provided a sense of clarity in highly complex and uncertain situations. Again, Hunter and colleagues found that pragmatic leaders demonstrated consistent performance across various conditions. Lovelace and Hunter (2013) created higher levels of perceived time pressure, which increases contextual demands on leaders, followers, and the organization (Bluedorn & Jaussi, 2008; Hunter et al., 2007; Shalley et al., 2004), to examine how the context changed influenced follower creative performance based on CIP leadership style. They found that the followers of charismatic and ideological leaders demonstrated performance declines in higher stress conditions, while followers of pragmatic leaders again showed consistent performance across conditions. Although the performance of CIP leaders in the aggregate reveals that there are multiple pathways to effective leadership, a review of the relevant empirical research indicates that CIP leader performance varies under key contextual conditions. As such, while there are multiple pathways to effective leadership, there is value in understanding how context can influence key outcomes of interest in CIP research.

Taken together, a steadily growing body of evidence supports the main propositions of the CIP leadership theory that (1) leadership styles differ based on individual mental models' structure and sensemaking approaches, (2) these differences in leadership styles result in variance in the decisions and behaviors of leaders, and (3) while there is nuance in specific outcomes that stem from leader differences, overall different CIP pathways can lead to outstanding outcomes overall.

4 Comparisons to Other Leadership Theories

To understand where the CIP leadership theory fits within the larger landscape of leadership research, it is important to consider similarities and differences of the CIP theory in relation to common, established, and emerging frameworks. Using an approach outlined by Brown and Trevino (2006), we discuss several of the most frequently studied leadership frameworks (Dinh et al., 2014), comparing and contrasting these approaches to the CIP theory. These similarities and differences are summarized in Table 4 and discussed in detail later.

4.1 Trait-Based Approach: Comparing to CIP

One of the oldest and historically most popular approaches to studying leadership is the trait-based approach (Carlyle, 1849; Galton, 1869). The trait-based approach to leadership proposes that there are qualities that differentiate leaders from non-leaders or successful leaders from unsuccessful leaders. Broadly, the study of traits and individual differences includes personality, needs, motives, values, and temperament (Yukl & Gardner, 2020). Commonly studied traits include, but are not limited to, intelligence (Ghiselli, 1963), locus of control (Miller & Toulouse, 1986), emotional maturity (Zhou & George, 2003), narcissism, extraversion (Bono & Judge, 2004), and conscientiousness. Zaccaro (2007) summarizes the trait-based approach to leadership and discusses a number of key aspects of the trait-based approach. In particular, Zaccaro discusses that one of the defining characteristics of the trait-based approach is stability. That is, because many traits are generally consistent in their manifestation over the span of a lifetime, they are predictive of leader effectiveness both longitudinally as well as across multiple contexts.

When comparing the trait-based approach to the CIP theory, it is clear that there is the degree of overlap. Broadly, both trait-based and CIP approaches stress the notion that characteristics of a leader impact leader behavior and, in

Table 4 Comparing CIP theory to popular leadership theories

Theory	Similarities to CIP	Differences from CIP
Trait-based	Both frameworks suggest that individual differences are key to understanding how leaders see the world and shape the world. Both approaches offer that there is some degree of stability in how individuals lead both longitudinally and across contexts.	For CIP, life experiences are central to understanding how leaders see the world and shape the world and are more critical to the theory than individual differences such as personality traits. Trait-based models implicitly stress that a set of qualities are required for the most effective approach to leading; CIP suggests that there are multiple ways to lead with one not being better than the other.
Dimensional models of leader behavior	CIP and the behavioral approach offer that there is variability in what behaviors are beneficial to leading. Although early models such as those at Ohio State suggested two dimensions, later behavioral models suggested three key sets of leader behavior that are consistent with the CIP framework.	Behavioral models implicitly or explicitly offer that effective leaders engage in all leader behaviors (i.e., one best way to lead); CIP stresses viability across various approaches. CIP stresses sensemaking approaches that are cognitively focused over the behavioral models that emphasize what leaders do, functionally.
Transformational	Findings on transformational leadership reveal that both transformational approaches and transactional approaches are linked to effective leadership suggesting that a range of approaches are beneficial for leading.	Although findings suggest that transactional behaviors are beneficial to effective leadership, the emergent message has been that transformational leadership is the *most* effective form of leadership; CIP argues for

Charismatic	Both CIP and transformational leadership recognize the appeal and utility of vision-based leading. Both CIP and charismatic leadership theories recognize the utility of a charismatic approach to leading that stress emotional appeals as core to leading.	equifinality across approaches countering the notion of "one best approach" to leading. Charismatic leadership suggests that there is one best or most effective manner of leading. CIP, in contrast, argues that the charismatic approach is only one of several effective forms of leading.
Leader–member exchange (LMX)	LMX and CIP both offer that leaders form unique relationship with followers and that there is variability in how some leaders connect with some followers. Both models emphasize relationships between leader and follower as central to understanding how leaders are able to accomplish goals as well as how those relationships evolve over time.	LMX emphasizes exchange relationships; CIP emphasizes sensemaking during ambiguous or complex contexts of leading.
Upper echelons theory (UET)	CIP and UET propose that a leader's view and perspective are shaped by a collection of experiences, values, and individual differences. UET and CIP both propose that a leader's worldview varies from leader to leader and has an impact on how they go about enacting their leadership approach.	UET does not specify pathways to leading; CIP offers that there are three primary pathways with the potential to have mixed pathways derived from a combination of these three. UET is primarily aimed at corporate leadership, CIP is a more general leadership theory aimed at multiple contexts.

particular, shape how individuals go about influencing others. That is, each leader possesses unique qualities that shape their approach to leading. Moreover, as outlined by Zaccaro (2007), the trait-based approach stresses stability longitudinally and situationally. Similarly, CIP theory proposes that although there is some variability in leadership styles as individuals experience significant life events, for most leaders, their style is crystalized in early adulthood (Mumford, 2006) and exhibit a consistent pattern across situations and life spans.

Despite these similarities, however, the trait-based approach and CIP differ in several ways. First, many traits are linked to genetic or inherited sources. Intelligence, for example, is highly heritable and also a consistent predictor of leader effectiveness (Bass & Bass, 2009). In contrast, the CIP theory centers on life experiences (Ligon et al., 2008) as drivers of the three leadership approaches. In addition, the trait-based approach holds that traits are predictive of leadership effectiveness. More intelligent leaders, for example, are more effective at leading. Leaders that are more emotionally mature are more effective leaders. The CIP theory, however, does not suggest that charismatic leadership is more effective than pragmatic or ideological leadership. Rather, each of these styles is *potential* pathway for effective leadership. That is, effectiveness is contingent upon how well each leader utilizes the pathway and how well followers resonate with that approach.

4.2 Dimensional Model of Leader Behavior: Comparing to CIP

As one set of leadership researchers set out to identify leadership traits (Stogdill, 1948), another group of researchers at Ohio State developed a set of survey items to investigate how often leaders engage in various leader behaviors (Fleischman, 1957). Similar efforts occurred at the University of Michigan (Likert, 1961) and Harvard as well (Bales, 1950) with all revealing that leadership behavior, when measured from the follower self-report perspective, could be summarized with two broad sets of behaviors. Although the labels and terminology varied, it became evident that when followers were asked what leaders did, these behaviors fell into the two dimensions of task and relationship behaviors (also called consideration and initiating structure; Fleischman, 1957). Task behaviors included organizing, planning, assigning, clarifying, and directing. Relationship behaviors included supporting, encouraging, coaching, consulting, resolving conflict, and informing (Yukl & Gardner, 2020). Moreover, the resulting belief regarding these behaviors was that effective leaders engaged in both task and relationship behaviors (Judge et al., 2004).

In considering similarities of the CIP theory and behavioral approach, it is apparent that the behavioral model of leadership has some interesting linkages to the CIP theory of leadership. First, the two-factor behavioral model emerging from work at Ohio State was one of the first to suggest that there were varying forms of leadership behavior or more generally, approaches to leading. That is, work from these groups of researchers revealed that there is not a singular set of leadership actions, but rather various dimensions of behavior linked to effectiveness. In fact, although the Ohio State and Michigan studies revealed two broad dimensions of leader behavior, Yukl and colleagues (2002) suggested a third category referred to as change behaviors. The case for three dimensions rather than two was made based on data collection efforts that utilized an expanded variant of the surveys used in the original Ohio State studies. Across several studies (Ekvall & Arvonen, 1991; Yukl, 1998), researchers found support for three dimensions rather than two. According to Yukl and Gardner (2020), task behaviors result in greater efficiency; relationship behaviors result in increased trust and identification; and change behavior results in greater innovation and transformation. Thus, the dimensional and resulting expansions of it map fairly well onto the styles of leadership defining the CIP theory that also offer similar responses from followers.

Although there are notable similarities between the CIP theory and the dimensional approach to leader behavior, there are also core differences. At a very basic level, the behavioral approach is focused on key behaviors a leader engages in, while the CIP model focuses on sensemaking via prescriptive and descriptive mental models. As such, the CIP model has substantial cognitive components in contrast to the behavioral focus of the two- and three-factor models. In addition, as is the case with the trait-based approach, the leader behavior models hold that as leaders engage in these behaviors, leader effectiveness increases. Taken further, the most effective leader is purported to engage in task and relationship behaviors. In contrast, the CIP model holds that leaders engage in their own unique stylistic approaches to leading and, in particular, to make sense of ambiguous contexts often characterizing the need for leadership. The behavioral approach offers prescriptive guidance on what effective leaders should do; the CIP theory emphasizes that there are multiple ways for a leader to reach outcomes successfully.

4.3 Transformational Leadership: Comparing to CIP

The most popular and heavily researched leadership theory of the modern era is transformational leadership (Dinh et al., 2014). Although not readily determined by the initial label of the theory, early work on transformational leadership drew a distinction between transformational leadership and transactional leadership. Transformational leadership (sometimes called transforming leadership) was aimed at drawing on moral values and energizing followers toward change (Yukl & Gardner, 2020). Transactional, on the other hand, was an exchange-oriented form of leadership, emphasizing a followers' self-interest (Burns, 1978). It is also of note that similar to Weber (1947), Burns (1978) suggested that there was a third approach to leading that emphasized tradition and custom. Burns' early work has given way to a range of variations, but the most popular has been that of Bass (1985) who suggested that transactional and transformational behaviors were linked to effective leadership but that transformational leadership was more effective in increasing motivation and performance. Transformational behaviors are theorized to fall into four dimensions (idealized influence, individualized consideration, inspirational motivation, and intellectual stimulation), which a leader uses to create a compelling vision that inspires followers. Meanwhile, transactional behaviors include three dimensions of behavior (contingent reward, management by exception passive, and management by exception active), which a leader generally uses to engage in punishment or reward behaviors to encourage compliance. Although criticized for a number of reasons (Van Knippenberg & Sitkin, 2013; Yukl, 1999), transformational leadership and transactional leadership are predictive of outcomes, such as motivation and performance (Lowe et al., 1996), and have developed a deep stream of research exploring these relationships.

The similarities and overlap of transformational leadership with the CIP model are notable. The first and most evident is that both theories recognize how impactful a compelling, future-oriented vision can be to followers. Transformational leadership cemented this premise, and CIP embraces the notion as a foundation as well. Both theoretical frameworks, moreover, suggest that in addition to an emotionally laden, inspirational approach to leading others there are other approaches to leading that are also linked to effective leadership. In some cases, transactional behaviors such as contingent reward are more predictive of performance than transformational behaviors such as a compelling vision (Vecchio et al., 2008) and provide further support for the notion of varying ways to lead.

Despite these similarities, transformational leadership and the CIP theory of leadership differ in several ways. Although there is variance across researchers in this notion, most advocates of transformational leadership emphasize utilizing transformational behaviors over transactional behaviors. That is, although transformational leadership acknowledges the importance of other behaviors beyond those falling under the rubric of transformational behavior, these dimensions are depicted as superior to transactional behaviors. In this sense, the theory contrasts CIP theory that embraces the principle of equifinality and suggests that each pathway is equally viable as an approach to leading. That is, transformational leadership emphasizes a narrower approach to leading successfully, while CIP embraces a more diverse and broader perspective. Furthermore, the origins of CIP are rooted in the cognition of the leader, not just behaviors. As such, CIP theory address many of the concerns about transformational leadership research (Lovelace et al., 2019). As such, the CIP framework better accounts for the process whereby leaders make sense of a situation and then take action to facilitate understanding and action by their followers. When comparing the CIP theory to transformational leadership, the theory is perhaps best depicted as acknowledging the critical work that has been done on transformational leadership but also proposes an expanded view of how leaders can successfully operate.

4.4 Charismatic Leadership: Comparing to CIP

The notion of charismatic leadership has been a source of debate and even consternation for some leadership researchers (Antonakis et al., 2016). Yet, similar to transformational leadership, charismatic leadership has been a heavily researched and popular framework for understanding how leaders influence others (Dinh et al., 2014; Lord et al., 2017). Although there are several variations, many have significant overlap with transformational leadership and, as such, offer that the reader refers to the previous discussion for these related frameworks. One framework that, from a conceptual standpoint, is unique enough to warrant discussion is the attribution model of charismatic leadership (Conger & Kanungo, 1988). The theory holds that leaders who offer a novel and engaging vision, emotionally appeal to core values, engage in unconventional behavior, appear confident, and are willing to engage in self-sacrifice are viewed as charismatic. That is, followers attribute charisma to these leaders and, as such, desire to be linked to, and associated with, that individual. Followers then personally identify with the leader and seek to imitate leader behavior and engage in actions to please the leader. A leader's influence is derived from this desire to identify and connect to the leader.

It is not surprising given the similarity between transformational and charismatic leadership that as a stand-alone theory, charismatic leadership has obvious linkage to the CIP theory. Even on the surface, the casual reader will note that the "C" in CIP also uses the label of charismatic. This surface-level linkage is reflective of more substantive connections as well, given that both theories emphasize an approach to leadership that is emotionally laden and compelling to followers. Moreover, both frameworks acknowledge and embrace the premise that an inspiring vision can be quite an effective way to engage followers.

As is the case with transformational leadership, however, charismatic leadership as a theory also contends that there is one effective approach to leading. Although not stated explicitly, the implication of the framework is that to be an effective leader, charismatic behavior and, by extension, attribution of charisma are necessary. More directly, in contrast to the CIP theory, the charismatic theory offers little room for other, alternative approaches to leading. Thus, although the two theories utilize similar labeling, there are fundamental differences in how they depict viable approaches to leading others.

4.5 Leader–Member Exchange: Comparing to CIP

The early version of LMX was referred to as the vertical dyad linkage (Dansereau et al., 1973). Although debated by some (e.g., Dienesch & Liden, 1986; Gottfredson et al., 2020), the basic premise of the theory is that leaders develop unique relationships with each follower. As expanded on later (Schriesheim et al., 1999), these relationships will vary in their quality or what is referred to as an exchange relationship. Higher quality relationships are built over time as followers demonstrate competence and dependability and leaders reciprocate with development and opportunity. Those with higher quality exchange relationships will receive greater attention, have influence via consultation, and receive increased benefits but are also expected to perform at a higher level and support the leader. LMX is a relationship-oriented theory that emphasizes the dynamic and unique interplay between leader and follower.

As alluded to previously, one of the most appealing characteristics of the LMX is that it focuses on relationships between leaders and followers rather than on traits or qualities of the leader. Leaders are also theorized to have unique relationships with each of their followers, and this variance is commensurate with the principles of CIP theory. That is, within the CIP theory, charismatic leaders will form relationships that differ from those formed with ideological and pragmatic leaders. In this sense, both theoretical frameworks acknowledge the unique and varying relationships followers can form with leaders. Moreover, later versions of LMX suggested that if followers viewed themselves as having a positive exchange relationship with their leader, that leader had greater influence over them (Graen & Uhl-Bien, 1995). This premise of building a connection to a leader is also foundational to CIP as well.

Despite such overlap, there are also a number of critical differences between the two theories. At a very basic level, LMX does not suggest or explore differing styles of leading and, instead, simply suggests that there are unique relationships between a leader and each follower. Moreover, CIP is grounded in the literature on sensemaking, with a leader offering one (or a combination) of pathways to help followers make sense of, and feel less ambiguity about, a given context. Within the CIP framework, should that attempt at sensemaking appeal to a follower, that leader is theorized to have greater influence over that follower. LMX, in contrast, focuses on exchanges between leader and follower without specifying sensemaking as a component of that exchange.

4.6 Upper Echelons Theory: Comparing to CIP

Dinh and colleagues (2014) summarized trends across leadership theories, with strategic leadership being recognized as an important area of investigation. With more than thirty-five years of research support, upper echelons theory (UET) stands out as one of the most commonly utilized and influential theories in the strategic leadership research landscape (Hambrick & Mason, 1984; Neely et al., 2020). It is not hard to understand the interest in examining the influence of executive orientation on firm outcomes given the significant impact CEOs have on firm outcomes (Quigley & Hambrick, 2015). As a baseline, UET proposes that executives in upper levels of an organization lead based on their own unique interpretations (i.e., individual orientation) of the situations they face and that these interpretations are driven by a combination of each executive's personal experiences, individual differences such as personality, and personal set of values (Hambrick, 2007; Hambrick & Mason, 1984; Neely et al., 2020). As an executive's orientation guides the way they see the world and make decisions for their firm, the organization increasingly becomes a reflection of the executive. For example, if the executive has a high propensity to take risks, the organization increasingly takes risky actions. Later versions of the theory were expanded to include additional variables like managerial discretion as key moderators, with executives that have more latitude of action having a greater influence on a firm's actions (Hambrick & Finkelstein, 1987). The basic idea is that when there is more uncertainty in the surrounding environment and there are fewer restrictions on the executive, a CEO's individual perspectives will have a greater impact on the decisions and actions of an organization. In addition, Hambrick and Mason (1984) stressed that decisions are made by the collection of top management teams or the aggregate of executives and not simply the CEO, although CEOs are often the focus of the theory (Carpenter et al., 2004; Hambrick, 2007). Several recent reviews provide useful summaries of the UET literature for additional information (see Bromiley & Rau, 2016; Neely et al., 2020; Wowak et al., 2017).

Although UET and strategic management more broadly are often siloed and held outside of the more traditional leadership literature, this gap is narrowing (Neely et al., 2020). Moreover, such bridge-building is seemingly quite useful, as the connections between UET and CIP are notable. First, both theories stress experiences, individual differences, and values as critical to shaping how a leader views the situations they face as well as the decisions that emerge from these worldviews. Implicit within UET is that leaders with differing experiences, values, and personalities can view the same situation differently and, as such, lead in differing ways. This core premise overlaps well with CIP in that both theories stress that these variables combine to drive varying approaches to leading. That is, neither CIP nor UET suggest that there is one best approach to leading.

Although there are a number of similarities between the two frameworks, the two approaches also differ in several ways as well. First, UET has historically been aimed at understanding CEOs and executive teams in the corporate world, whereas CIP is a more general leadership theory, aimed at a broader range of leaders. Second, UET proposes that each leader develops a unique lens with which to view the world but does not specify the leadership approaches that can emerge from such lenses. That is, whereas CIP proposes three primary pathways, UET offers an unspecified number of approaches that emerge from characteristics and attributes possessed by leaders. Finally, CIP focuses on the means by which the leadership styles result in follower influence. That is, followers are a primary focus in the theory, whereas UET emphasizes organizational outcomes at the organizational unit of analysis.

To summarize, CIP theory is related to a number of popular and heavily researched theories. The theory embraces the notion that some leaders are effective by using an emotionally evocative vision, for example, as do theories such as transformational and charismatic leadership. Moreover, CIP theory suggests that individual differences and life experiences drive how leaders see the world, much like UET and other theories such as trait-based leadership. CIP theory also offers that differing leaders will form unique relationships with followers, a central component of LMX. Despite such overlap, the theory is also unique in its emphasis on equifinality or varying pathways to leading. Moreover, the framework emphasizes the unique relationships each pathway forms with followers, embracing the notion that not all followers are homogeneous, and each has their own views about whether a given leadership approach will result in outcomes they desire. In many ways, CIP embraces many of the proven and established components of previous theories while also offering unique elements to expand the leadership space.

5 Summary and Future Directions

Grounded in concepts from Weber (1947), the CIP theory of leadership took a more concrete form in work by Mumford (2006) and has been investigated across more than fifteen years and twenty-five studies (Allen et al., 2020). Although the findings are complex and span a range of methods and outcomes, the body of work can be summarized with three strengths that contribute most substantively to the study and understanding of leadership. The first is that the framework embodies the principle of diversity and diverse pathways to leadership. Although not focused on the diversity literature directly (more on this later in the Element), the CIP theory is principally commensurate with the notion that there is no "one best way" to lead. Framed differently, CIP emphasizes that leadership can take diverse forms and there is equality in the ability to achieve success as a leader (Hunter & Lovelace, 2020). One implication, observed in our experiences talking to current and emerging leaders, is that those individuals who do not feel they fit the prescribed mold for being a leader can begin to see themselves as leaders via the CIP approach. More directly stated, we have both witnessed firsthand that a larger proportion of individuals see themselves as potential leaders when they are exposed to the principles of the CIP model. We see this as one of the theory's simplest but most meaningful contributions.

The second way the theory has meaningfully contributed to our understanding of leadership is through embracing both follower and leader perspectives. In particular, the CIP theory emphasizes that followers look to leaders for sensemaking in complex and ambiguous contexts and that followers will respond differently to varying sensemaking attempts. Followers, in this sense, are not characterized as passive recipients of the leaders' will, but rather are unique in what they prefer in a leader (Thoroughgood et al., 2020). More importantly, these preferences will result in differing responses to leader attempts at sensemaking. This nuance and acknowledgment that followers are unique, diverse, and heterogeneous (Uhl-Bien et al., 2014) allow the theory to capture the complexity that comprises leader and follower dynamics.

Third and finally, the CIP theory has contributed to our understanding of leadership by acknowledging the role that experiences play in shaping our unique worldviews as leaders and as followers. It is no surprise that the CIP model is grounded in a life experience approach given Mumford's prior work on biodata and experience as a predictor of performance (e.g., Mumford et al., 2012; Stokes et al., 1994). Moreover, because the theory was initially formed from the use of historiometric data or content analysis of a leader's life (Crayne & Hunter, 2018), the leader's full life experience was incorporated into the framing and conceptualization of the theory. Although consistent with other theories such as UET

(Hambrick & Mason, 1984), this premise of life experience and individual differences providing a unique lens through which leaders view the world is rather unique in the leadership literature more broadly (Zaccarro et al., 2018). Such experiences, moreover, are not predicted to be superior or inferior to one another. Rather, as CIP suggests, how each of us reaches success may vary, but each pathway is a viable route to achievement.

5.1 Future Research

Despite the strengths and contributions of the CIP theory, there remain critical areas for advancement and improvement. Moving forward, we see three primary areas those studying the CIP theory should focus on. First, although the framework is grounded in the principle of diversity, or variability in the pathways to leadership, the CIP theory is just now advancing with regard to explicit predictions on the various forms of diversity. In their recent work on gender and the CIP theory, for example, Griffith and Medeiros (2020) make several propositions on the role of gender in shaping future development and refinement of the CIP theory. Areas to consider include the unique experiences women face when forming leadership mental models as well as the often-limited set of leader behaviors viewed as acceptable by subordinates. It will be critical that the theory continues to work along these lines and begins to incorporate other surfaces (e.g., demographic) and deep level (e.g., expertise) differences among leaders to ensure applicability to all leaders. Moreover, adaptations and refinement will be necessary if such applicability is not observed.

In addition to expanding our understanding of diversity and the CIP theory, it will be critical that future researchers continue to expand on the premise of nuance among the three pathways. That is, although the CIP theory was originally conceptualized as being composed of three primary pathways, it is clear that leaders have within-leader variability in their utilization of these pathways. Barack Obama, for example, is clearly a charismatic leader with his promise of hope as a central message, yet the former president also exhibited signs of pragmatism in the execution of his agenda. The three leaders discussed at the outset of this Element; moreover, each represents illustrations of the CIP pathways, yet inspection of their approaches to leading reveals nuanced variability across each of the three styles. Anne Wojcicki, for example, exhibits a strongly pragmatic style of leading yet also is lauded for her vision and ability to enact change through her infectious enthusiasm. In other words, she also exhibits a charismatic style in some contexts. This nuance is one of the reasons that researchers (e.g., Hunter & Lovelace, 2020; Lovelace et al., 2019) have begun to suggest that advanced approaches to considering the three pathways may lead to a greater and richer understanding of how each leader influences followers. It is essential that future research continue to consider the nuance in leader approaches while balancing the intuitive appeal of the three pathway categories (Lascano et al., 2020).

One final area for future research is in the advancement of practical application. The vast majority of work on the CIP theory has been aimed at understanding the three pathways and their linkages to key performance outcomes. Put another way, the work has been largely academically oriented. Limited work, in contrast, has been aimed at considering how to most effectively use and apply this improved understanding in a practical sense (see Lascano et al., 2020). With regard to practical application, specifically, we see a few basic areas for future consideration. First, given advancements in measurement (Lovelace et al., 2020), it is now feasible to provide leaders with an assessment of their CIP profile. Such an advancement is not trivial as the sound measurement is a precursor to substantive development in both research and practice. Second, with a profile afforded due to improvements in measurement, it will be possible to provide leaders with guidance on how to most effectively utilize their style of leadership. Leaders can be provided with information on how followers are likely to respond and how those responses may help improve performance and subordinate well-being. Along related lines, leaders can also be provided with potential pitfalls linked to each pathway. Those utilizing a charismatic pathway, for example, may be warned that excessive emotional appeals can lead to burnout (Yukl, 1999). Leaders using a pragmatic pathway may be informed that their approach may take time to engage and convince followers and they should be aware of the investment required to see results (e.g., Lovelace & Hunter, 2013). Third and finally, when given insight into their own style of leading, leaders may choose to develop support teams with complimentary styles. A pragmatic leader, for example, may add leaders more charismatically and ideologically oriented to help round out their ability to manage a diverse swath of subordinates.

5.2 Concluding Comments

The CIP theory of leadership is an expansive framework for understanding how leaders uniquely influence followers. The theory utilizes key components from established models of leadership and offers additional, novel pathways to performance. A key feature of the framework is allowing a wider range of individuals to see themselves as potential leaders and encouraging those who may not initially view themselves as capable of leading others effectively. Although the theory is more than fifteen years old and research has been largely supportive of the framework, much work remains, and future avenues for research are just now beginning to emerge.

References

Allen, J. B., Lovelace, J. B., Hunter, S. T., & Neely, B. (2020). Foundations of the CIP theory: An overview. In S. T. Hunter & J. B. Lovelace (Eds.), *Multiple pathways to outstanding leadership: Revisiting CIP theory* (pp. 22–47). New York: Routledge.

Anderson, S. J., & Conway, M. A. (1993). Investigating the structure of autobiographical memories. *Journal of Experimental Psychology: Learning, Memory, and Cognition, 19*(5), 1178.

Antonakis, J., Bastardoz, N., Jacquart, P., & Shamir, B. (2016). Charisma: An ill-defined and ill-measured gift. *Annual Review of Organizational Psychology and Organizational Behavior, 3*, 293–319.

Antonakis, J., & Day, D. V. (2018). Leadership: Past, present, and future. In J. Antonakis & D. V. Day (Eds.), *The nature of leadership* (pp. 3–26). California: Sage.

Ashmos, D. P., & Huber, G. P. (1987). The systems paradigm in organization theory: Correcting the record and suggesting the future. *Academy of Management Review, 12*, 607–621.

Atwater, L. E., Dionne, S. D., Avolio, B., Camobreco, J. E., & Lau, A. W. (1999). A longitudinal study of the leadership development process: Individual differences predicting leader effectiveness. *Human Relations, 52* (12), 1543–1562.

Baas, M., Roskes, M., Sligte, D., Nijstad, B. A., & De Dreu, C. K. (2013). Personality and creativity: The dual pathway to creativity model and a research agenda. *Social and Personality Psychology Compass, 7*(10), 732–748.

Babcock-Roberson, M. E., & Strickland, O. J. (2010). The relationship between charismatic leadership, work engagement, and organizational citizenship behaviors. *The Journal of Psychology, 144*, 313–326.

Bakker, A. B., Demerouti, E., & Sanz-Vergel, A. I. (2014). Burnout and work engagement: The JD–R approach. *Annual Review of Organizational Psychology and Organizational Behavior, 1*, 389–411.

Bales, R. F. (1950). A set of categories for the analysis of small group interaction. *American Sociological Review, 15*(2), 257–263.

Barnard, C. (1938). *The functions of the executive*. Cambridge: Harvard University Press.

Bass, B. M. (1985). *Leadership and performance beyond expectations*. New York: Collier Macmillan.

Bass, B. M., & Bass, R. (2009).*The Bass handbook of leadership: Theory, research, and managerial applications*. New York: Simon and Schuster.

Bedell, K., Hunter, S., Angie, A., & Vert, A. (2006). A historiometric examination of Machiavellianism and a new taxonomy of leadership. *Journal of Leadership & Organizational Studies, 12*(4), 50–72.

Bedell-Avers, K., Hunter, S. T., Angie, A. D., Eubanks, D. L., & Mumford, M. D. (2009). Charismatic, ideological, and pragmatic leaders: An examination of leader–leader interactions. *The Leadership Quarterly, 20*(3), 299–315.

Bedell-Avers, K. E., Hunter, S. T., & Mumford, M. D. (2008). Conditions of problem-solving and the performance of charismatic, ideological, and pragmatic leaders: A comparative experimental study. *The Leadership Quarterly, 19*, 89–106.

Bennis, W. G., & Thomas, R. J. (2002). *Geeks and geezers: How era, values, and defining moments shape leaders-how tough times shape good leaders*. Boston, MA: Harvard Business School.

Bledow, R., Frese, M., Anderson, N., Erez, M., & Farr, J. (2009). A dialectic perspective on innovation: Conflicting demands, multiple pathways, and ambidexterity. *Industrial and Organizational Psychology, 2*(3), 305–337.

Bluedorn, A. C., & Jaussi, K. S. (2008). Leaders, followers, and time. *The Leadership Quarterly, 19*(6), 654–668.

Boal, K. B., & Hooijberg, R. (2000). Strategic leadership research: Moving on. *The Leadership Quarterly, 11*(4), 515–549.

Bono, J. E., Foldes, H. J., Vinson, G., & Muros, J. P. (2007). Workplace emotions: The role of supervision and leadership. *Journal of Applied Psychology, 92*(5), 1357–1367.

Bono, J. E., & Ilies, R. (2006). Charisma, positive emotions and mood contagion. *The Leadership Quarterly, 17*(4), 317–334.

Bono, J. E., & Judge, T. A. (2004). Personality and transformational and transactional leadership: A meta-analysis. *Journal of Applied Psychology, 89*(5), 901–910.

Brescoll, V. L. (2016). Leading with their hearts? How gender stereotypes of emotion lead to biased evaluations of female leaders. *The Leadership Quarterly, 27*(3), 415–428.

Brescoll, V. L., Okimoto, T. G., & Vial, A. C. (2018). You've come a long way ... maybe: How moral emotions trigger backlash against women leaders. *Journal of Social Issues, 74*(1), 144–164.

Bromiley, P., & Rau, D. (2016). Social, behavioral, and cognitive influences on upper echelons during strategy process: A literature review. *Journal of Management, 42*(1), 174–202.

Brown, A. D., Colville, I., & Pye, A. (2015). Making sense of sensemaking in organization studies. *Organization Studies, 36*(2), 265–277.

Brown, M. E., & Trevino, L. K. (2006). Ethical leadership: A review and future directions. *The Leadership Quarterly, 17*(6), 595–616.

Burke, P. (2005). *History and social theory.* Oxford: Cornell University Press.

Burns, J. M. (1978). *Leadership.* New York: Harper and Row.

Carlyle, T. (1849). *On heroes, hero-worship, and the heroic in history.* Boston, MA: Houghton-Mifflin.

Carpenter, M. A., Geletkanycz, M. A., & Sanders, W. G. (2004). Upper echelons research revisited: Antecedents, elements, and consequences of top management team composition. *Journal of Management, 30,* 749–778.

Carter, S. (2016, January 12). A day in the life of Anne Wojcicki. *Wall Street Journal.* https://www.wsj.com/articles/a-day-in-the-life-of-anne-wojcicki-1452613783.

Chhokar, J. S., Brodbeck, F. C., & House, R. J. (Eds.). (2007). *Culture and leadership across the world: The GLOBE book of in-depth studies of 25 societies.* New York: Routledge.

Christian, M. S., Garza, A. S., & Slaughter, J. E. (2011). Work engagement: A quantitative review and test of its relations with task and contextual performance. *Personnel Psychology, 64*(1), 89–136.

Conger, J. A., & Kanungo, R. N. (1988). The empowerment process: Integrating theory and practice. *Academy of Management Review, 13,* 471–482.

Crayne, M. P., & Hunter, S. T. (2018). Historiometry in organizational science: Renewed attention for an established research method. *Organizational Research Methods, 21*(1), 6–29.

Crayne, M. P., & Medeiros, K. E. (2020). Making sense of crisis: Charismatic, ideological, and pragmatic leadership in response to COVID-19. *American Psychologist, 76*(3), 462–474.

Cyert, R. M., & March, J. G. (1963). *A behavioral theory of the firm* (Vol. 2, pp. 169–187). Englewood Cliffs: Prentice Hall.

Dansereau, F., Cashman, J., & Graen, G. (1973). Instrumentality theory and equity theory as complementary approaches in predicting the relationship of leadership and turnover among managers. *Organizational Behavior and Human Performance, 10*(2), 184–200.

Day, D. V., Fleenor, J. W., Atwater, L. E., Sturm, R. E., & McKee, R. A. (2014). Advances in leader and leadership development: A review of 25 years of research and theory. *The Leadership Quarterly, 25*(1), 63–82.

DeRue, D. S., Nahrgang, J. D., Wellman, N. E. D., & Humphrey, S. E. (2011). Trait and behavioral theories of leadership: An integration and meta-analytic test of their relative validity. *Personnel Psychology, 64,* 7–52.

Dienesch, R. M., & Liden, R. C. (1986). Leader-member exchange model of leadership: A critique and further development. *Academy of Management Review, 11*(3), 618–634.

Dinh, J. E., Lord, R. G., Gardner, W. L. et al. (2014). Leadership theory and research in the new millennium: Current theoretical trends and changing perspectives. *The Leadership Quarterly, 25*, 36–62.

Ekvall, G., & Arvonen, J. (1991). Change-centered leadership: An extension of the two-dimensional model. *Scandinavian Journal of Management, 7*(1), 17–26.

Finkelstein, S., Hambrick, D. C., & Cannella Jr, A. A. (2009). *Strategic leadership: Theory and research on executives, top management teams, and boards*. New York: Oxford University Press.

Fleischman, E. A. (1957). A leader behavior description for industry. In R. M. Stogdill & A. E. Coons (Eds.), *Leader behavior: Its description and measurement* (pp. 10–119). Columbus: Bureau of Business Research, Ohio State University.

Fredrickson, B. L. (2001). The role of positive emotions in positive psychology: The broaden-and-build theory of positive emotions. *American Psychologist, 56*(3), 218.

Fromm, E. (1973). *The anatomy of human destructiveness*. New York: Holt, Rinehart, & Winston.

Galton, F. (1869). *Hereditary genius*. New York: Appleton.

George, J. M. (2000). Emotions and leadership: The role of emotional intelligence. *Human Relations, 53*(8), 1027–1055.

Ghiselli, E. E. (1963). Intelligence and managerial success. *Psychological Reports, 12*(3), 898.

Gioia, D. A., & Chittipeddi, K. (1991). Sensemaking and sensegiving in strategic change initiation. *Strategic Management Journal, 12*(6), 433–448.

Gioia, D. A., & Poole, P. P. (1984). Scripts in organizational behavior. *Academy of Management Review, 9*(3), 449–459.

Goldvarg, E., & Johnson-Laird, P. N. (2001). Naive causality: A mental model theory of causal meaning and reasoning. *Cognitive Science, 25*(4), 565–610.

Gottfredson, R. K., Wright, S. L., & Heaphy, E. D. (2020). A critique of the leader-member exchange construct: Back to square one. *The Leadership Quarterly, 31*(6), 1–17.

Graen, G. B., & Uhl-Bien, M. (1995). Relationship-based approach to leadership: Development of leader-member exchange (LMX) theory of leadership over 25 years: Applying a multi-level multi-domain perspective. *The Leadership Quarterly, 6*(2), 219–247.

Gresov, C., & Drazin, R. (1997). Equifinality: Functional equivalence in organization design. *Academy of Management Review, 22*(2), 403–428.

Griffith, J., Connelly, S., Thiel, C., & Johnson, G. (2015). How outstanding leaders lead with affect: An examination of charismatic, ideological, and pragmatic leaders. *The Leadership Quarterly, 26*, 502–517.

Griffith, J. A., Gibson, C., Medeiros, K. et al. (2018). Are you thinking what I'm thinking? The influence of leader style, distance, and leader–follower mental model congruence on creative performance. *Journal of Leadership and Organizational Studies, 25*, 153–170.

Griffith, J. A., & Medeiros, K. E. (2020). Gender (under) representation in the CIP model: Reconsidering outstanding leadership through a gender lens. In *Extending the Charismatic, Ideological, and Pragmatic Approach to Leadership* (pp. 200–224). New York: Routledge.

Habermas, T., & Bluck, S. (2000). Getting a life: The emergence of the life story in adolescence. *Psychological Bulletin, 126*(5), 748–769.

Hackman, J. R., & Wageman, R. (2007). Asking the right questions about leadership: Discussion and conclusions. *American Psychologist, 62*, 43–47.

Hall, D. T. (2004). Self-awareness, identity, and leader development. In D. V. Day, S. J. Zaccaro, & S. M. Halpin (Eds.), *Leader development for transforming organizations: Growing leaders for tomorrow* (pp. 153–176). Mahwah, NJ: Erlbaum.

Hambrick, D. C. (1989). Guest editor's introduction: Putting top managers back in the strategy picture. *Strategic Management Journal, 10*, 5–15.

Hambrick, D. C. (2007). Upper echelons theory: An update. *Academy of Management Review, 32*(2), 334–343.

Hambrick, D. C., & Finkelstein, S. (1987). Managerial discretion: A bridge between polar views of organizational outcomes. *Research in Organizational Behavior, 9*, 369–406.

Hambrick, D. C., & Mason, P. A. (1984). Upper echelons: The organization as a reflection of its top managers. *Academy of Management Review, 9*(2), 193–206.

Hammond, M., Clapp-Smith, R., & Palanski, M. (2017). Beyond (just) the workplace: A theory of leader development across multiple domains. *Academy of Management Review, 42*(3), 481–498.

Haslam, S. A., Reicher, S. D., Millard, K., & McDonald, R. (2015). "Happy to have been of service": The Yale archive as a window into the engaged followership of participants in Milgram's "obedience" experiments. *British Journal of Social Psychology, 54*, 55–83.

Helmreich, R. L. (1979). Social psychology on the flight deck. *Paper presented at the NASA Workshop on Resource Management Training for Airline Flight Crews*, San Francisco.

Hiller, N. J., DeChurch, L. A., Murase, T., & Doty, D. (2011). Searching for outcomes of leadership: A 25-year review. *Journal of Management, 37,* 1137–1177.

Hooijberg, R., Hunt, J. G., & Dodge, G. E. (1997). Leadership complexity and development of the leaderplex model. *Journal of Management, 23*(3), 375–408.

House, R. J., & Howell, J. M. (1992). Personality and charismatic leadership. *The Leadership Quarterly, 3*(2), 81–108.

Hunter, S. T., Bedell-Avers, K. E., & Mumford, M. D. (2007). The typical leadership study: Assumptions, implications, and potential remedies. *The Leadership Quarterly, 18*(5), 435–446.

Hunter, S. T., Bedell-Avers, K. E., & Mumford, M. D. (2009). Impact of situational framing and complexity on charismatic, ideological and pragmatic leaders: Investigation using a computer simulation. *The Leadership Quarterly, 20,* 383–404.

Hunter, S. T., Cushenbery, L., Thoroughgood, C. N., & Ligon, G. S. (2011). First and ten leadership: A historiometric investigation of the CIP leadership model. *The Leadership Quarterly, 22,* 70–91.

Hunter, S. T., & Lovelace, J. B. (Eds.). (2020). *Extending the charismatic, ideological, and pragmatic approach to leadership: Multiple pathways to success.* New York: Routledge.

Janis, I. L. (1954). Personality correlates of susceptibility to persuasion. *Journal of Personality, 22*(4), 504–518.

Janson, A. (2008). Extracting leadership knowledge from formative experiences. *Leadership, 4*(1), 73–94.

Johnson, S. K. (2008). I second that emotion: Effects of emotional contagion and affect at work on leader and follower outcomes. *The Leadership Quarterly, 19,* 1–19.

Joshi, A., & Knight, A. P. (2015). Who defers to whom and why? Dual pathways linking demographic differences and dyadic deference to team effectiveness. *Academy of Management Journal, 58*(1), 59–84.

Judge, T. A., Piccolo, R. F., & Ilies, R. (2004). The forgotten ones? The validity of consideration and initiating structure in leadership research. *Journal of Applied Psychology, 89*(1), 36–51.

Katz, D., & Kahn, R. L. (1978). *The social psychology of organizations* (Vol. 2). New York: Wiley.

Kotlyar, I., Karakowsky, L., & Ng, P. (2011). Leader behaviors, conflict and member commitment to team-generated decisions. *The Leadership Quarterly, 22,* 666–679.

Kotter, J. P. (1988). *The leadership factor.* New York: Free Press.

Lascano, J. J., Boatman, P., Strange, J. M., & Walters, K. W. (2020). Beyond outstanding to everyday: An applied perspective. In S.T. Hunter & J. B. Lovelace (Eds.), *Extending the charismatic, ideological, and pragmatic approach to leadership: Multiple pathways to success*. New York: Routledge.

Ligon, G. S., Harris, D. J., & Hunter, S. T. (2012). Quantifying leader lives: What historiometric approaches can tell us. *The Leadership Quarterly, 23*, 1104–1133.

Ligon, G. S., Hunter, S. T., & Mumford, M. D. (2008). Development of outstanding leadership: A life narrative approach. *The Leadership Quarterly, 19*(3), 312–334.

Likert, R. (1961). *New patterns of management*. New York: McGraw-Hill.

Lord, R. G., Day, D. V., Zaccaro, S. J., Avolio, B. J., & Eagly, A. H. (2017). Leadership in applied psychology: Three waves of theory and research. *Journal of Applied Psychology, 102*(3), 434.

Lovelace, J. B., & Hunter, S. T. (2013). Charismatic, ideological, and pragmatic leaders' influence on subordinate creative performance across the creative process. *Creativity Research Journal, 25*, 59–74.

Lovelace, J. B., Hunter, S. T., & Neely, B. H. (2020). Advancing the CIP model of leadership: A scale development effort. In S. T. Hunter & J. B. Lovelace (Eds.), *Multiple pathways to outstanding leadership: Revisiting CIP theory* (pp. 78–115). New York: Routledge.

Lovelace, J. B., Neely, B. H., Allen, J. B., & Hunter, S. T. (2019). Charismatic, ideological, & pragmatic (CIP) model of leadership: A critical review and agenda for future research. *The Leadership Quarterly, 30*(1), 96–110.

Lovelace, J. B., Neely, B. H., Jayne, B. S., & Hunter, S. T. (2017). All roads lead to Rome: Navigating the creative process using the CIP model of leadership. In M. Mumford & S. Hemlin (Eds.), *The handbook of research on leadership and creativity* (pp. 316–339). Northampton, MA: Edward Elgar.

Lowe, K. B., Kroeck, K. G., & Sivasubramaniam, N. (1996). Effectiveness correlates of transformational and transactional leadership: A meta-analytic review of the MLQ literature. *The Leadership Quarterly, 7*(3), 385–425.

Lubart, T. I. (2001). Models of the creative process: Past, present and future. *Creativity Research Journal, 13*(3–4), 295–308.

Maitlis, S., & Christianson, M. (2014). Sensemaking in organizations: Taking stock and moving forward. *Academy of Management Annals, 8*, 57–125.

Maitlis, S., & Lawrence, T. B. (2007). Triggers and enablers of sensegiving in organizations. *Academy of Management Journal, 50*, 57–84.

March, J. G., & Simon, H. A. (1958). *Organizations*. Oxford: Wiley.

McAdams, D. P. (2006). *The redemptive self: Stories Americans live by*. New York: Oxford University Press.

Miles, R. E., Snow, C. C., Meyer, A. D., & Coleman Jr, H. J. (1978). Organizational strategy, structure, and process. *Academy of Management Review*, *3*(3), 546–562.

Milgram, S. (1963). Behavioral study of obedience. *The Journal of Abnormal and Social Psychology*, *67*, 371–378.

Miller, D., & Toulouse, J. M. (1986). Chief executive personality and corporate strategy and structure in small firms. *Management Science*, *32*(11), 1389–1409.

Mischel, W. (1977). The interaction of person and situation. In D. Magnusson &N. S. Endler (Eds.), *Personality at the crossroads: Current issues in interactional psychology* (pp. 333–352). Hillsdale: Lawrence Erlbaum Associates.

Mobley, M. I., Doares, L. M., & Mumford, M. D. (1992). Process analytic models of creative capacities: Evidence for the combination and reorganization process. *Creativity Research Journal*, *5*(2), 125–155.

Mumford, M. D. (2002). Social innovation: Ten cases from Benjamin Franklin. *Creativity Research Journal*, *14*(2), 253–266.

Mumford, M. D. (2006). *Pathways to outstanding leadership: A comparative analysis of charismatic, ideological, and pragmatic Leaders*. Mahwah, NJ: Lawrence Erlbaum.

Mumford, M. D., Antes, A. L., Caughron, J. J., & Friedrich, T. L. (2008). Charismatic, ideological, and pragmatic leadership: Multi-level influences on emergence and performance. *The Leadership Quarterly*, *19*(2), 144–160.

Mumford, M. D., Barrett, J. D., & Hester, K. S. (2012). 16 background data: Use of experiential knowledge in personnel selection. In *The Oxford handbook of personnel assessment and selection* (pp. 353–382). Oxford: Oxford University Press.

Mumford, M. D., Bedell, K. E., Hunter, S. T., Espejo, J., & Boatman, P. R. (2006a). Problem solving-turning crises into opportunities: How charismatic, ideological, and pragmatic leaders solve problems. In M. D. Mumford (Ed.), *Pathways to outstanding leadership: A comparative analysis of charismatic, ideological, and pragmatic leadership* (pp. 108–137). Mahwah, NJ: Lawrence Erlbaum.

Mumford, M. D., Bedell, K. E., & Scott, G. M. (2006b). Developmental influences – What kind of leader are you destined to be? In M. D. Mumford (Ed.), *Pathways to outstanding leadership: A comparative analysis of charismatic, ideological, and pragmatic leadership* (pp. 246–267). Mahwah, NJ: Erlbaum Press.

Mumford, M. D., Connelly, M. S., Helton, W. B., Van Doorn, J. R., & Osburn, H. K. (2002). Alternative approaches for measuring values: Direct and indirect assessments in performance prediction. *Journal of Vocational Behavior*, *61*(2), 348–373.

Mumford, M. D., Espejo, J., Hunter, S. T. et al. (2007). The sources of leader violence: A comparison of ideological and non-ideological leaders. *The Leadership Quarterly, 18*(3), 217–235.

Mumford, M. D., Gaddis, B., Licuanan, B., Ersland, B., & Siekel, K. (2006c). Communication strategies – Persuasion or logic: How do outstanding leaders connect with their followers? In M. D. Mumford (Ed.), *Pathways to outstanding leadership: A comparative analysis of charismatic, ideological, and pragmatic leadership* (pp. 167–189). Mahwah, NJ: Lawrence Erlbaum.

Mumford, M. D., Licuanan, B., Marcy, R. T., Dailey, L., & Blair, C. (2006d). Political tactics getting ahead: How charismatic, ideological, and pragmatic leaders use influence tactics. In M. D. Mumford (Ed.), *Pathways to outstanding leadership: A comparative analysis of charismatic, ideological, and pragmatic leadership* (pp. 190–214). Mahwah, NJ: Erlbaum Press.

Mumford, M. D., Mobley, M. I., Uhlman, C. E., Reiter-Palmon, R., & Doares, L. M. (1991). Process analytic models of creative capacities. *Creativity Research Journal, 4*, 91–122.

Mumford, M. D., Scott, G., & Hunter, S. T. (2006e). Theory – Charismatic, ideological, and pragmatic leaders: How do they lead, why do they lead, and who do they lead? In M. D. Mumford (Ed.), *Pathways to outstanding leadership: A comparative analysis of charismatic, ideological, and pragmatic leadership* (pp. 25–51). Mahwah, NJ: Erlbaum Press.

Mumford, M. D., Scott, G. M., Marcy, R. T., Tutt, M. J., & Espejo, J. (2006f). Development – What early life experiences prepare you for outstanding leadership? In M. D. Mumford (Ed.), *Pathways to outstanding leadership: A comparative analysis of charismatic, ideological, and pragmatic leadership* (pp. 215–245). Mahwah: Erlbaum Press.

Mumford, M. D., Standish, C., & Gujar, Y. (2020). The charismatic, ideological, and pragmatic leadership model: Origins, findings, directions, and limitations. In S. T. Hunter & J. B. Lovelace (Eds.), *Multiple pathways to outstanding leadership: Revisiting CIP theory* (pp. 1–21). New York: Routledge.

Mumford, M. D., Strange, J. M., Scott, G. M., & Gaddis, B. (2004). Creative problem-solving in leadership: Directions, actions and reactions. *Creativity across domains: Faces of the muse* (pp. 205–223). Mahwah, NJ: Lawrence Erlbaum Associates, Inc

Mumford, M. D., Strange, J. M., Gaddis, B., Licuanan, B., & Scott, G. (2006g). Performance: Who masters the art of influence? Charismatic, ideological, or pragmatic leaders? In M. D. Mumford (Ed.), *Pathways to outstanding leadership: A comparative analysis of charismatic, ideological, and pragmatic leadership* (pp. 81–107). Mahwah: Lawrence Erlbaum.

Mumford, M. D., Strange, J. M., Scott, G. M., Dailey, L., & Blair, C. (2006h). Leader-follower interactions – Heroes, leaders, and tyrants: How do they relate? In M. D. Mumford (Ed.), *Pathways to outstanding leadership: A comparative analysis of charismatic, ideological, and pragmatic leadership* (pp. 138–166). Mahwah: Erlbaum Press.

Mumford, M. D., & Van Doorn, J. R. (2001). The leadership of pragmatism: Reconsidering Franklin in the age of charisma. *The Leadership Quarterly, 12* (3), 279–309.

Nadkarni, S., & Narayanan, V. K. (2007). Strategic schemas, strategic flexibility, and firm performance: The moderating role of industry clockspeed. *Strategic Management Journal, 28*(3), 243–270.

Neely Jr, B. H., Lovelace, J. B., Cowen, A. P., & Hiller, N. J. (2020). Metacritiques of upper echelons theory: Verdicts and recommendations for future research. *Journal of Management, 46*(6), 1029–1062.

Pillemer, D. B. (2001). Momentous events and the life story. *Review of General Psychology, 5*(2), 123–134.

Porac, J. F., & Thomas, H. (2002). Managing cognition and strategy: Issues, trends and future directions. In A. M. Pettigrew, H. Thomas, and R. Whittington (Eds.), *Handbook of strategy and management* (pp. 165–181). Thousand Oaks: Sage.

Porter, M. E. (1980). *Competitive strategy: Techniques for analyzing industries and competitors*. New York: Free Press.

Quigley, T. J., & Hambrick, D. C. (2015). Has the "CEO effect" increased in recent decades? A new explanation for the great rise in America's attention to corporate leaders. *Strategic Management Journal, 36*, 821–830.

Ryan, K. D. (2019, March). 23andMe's Anne Wojcicki says doing these 2 things as a leader built her company's culture of honesty. *Inc. Magazine.* https://www.inc.com/magazine/201904/kevin-j-ryan/23andme-anne-wojcicki-best-business-advice.html.

Schriesheim, C. A., Castro, S. L., & Cogliser, C. C. (1999). Leader-member exchange (LMX) research: A comprehensive review of theory, measurement, and data-analytic practices. *The Leadership Quarterly, 10*(1), 63–113.

Shalley, C. E., & Gilson, L. L. (2004). What leaders need to know: A review of social and contextual factors that can foster or hinder creativity. *The Leadership Quarterly, 15*(1), 33–53.

Stogdill, R. M. (1948). Personal factors associated with leadership: A survey of the literature. *Journal of Psychology, 25*, 35–71.

Stokes, G. S., Mumford, M. D., & Owens, W. A. (1994). *Biodata handbook: Theory, research, and use of biographical information in selection and performance prediction*. Palo Alto: CPP Books.

Strange, J. M., & Mumford, M. D. (2002). The origins of vision: Charismatic versus ideological leadership. *The Leadership Quarterly, 13*(4), 343–377.

Strange, J. M., & Mumford, M. D. (2005). The origins of vision: Effects of reflection, models, and analysis. *The Leadership Quarterly, 16*(1), 121–148.

Streufert, S., Streufert, S. C., & Castore, C. H. (1968). Leadership in negotiations and the complexity of conceptual structure. *Journal of Applied Psychology, 52*(3), 218–223.

Stürmer, S., & Simon, B. (2004). Collective action: Towards a dual-pathway model. *European Review of Social Psychology, 15*(1), 59–99.

Suedfelt, P., & Tetlock, P. E. (2014). Integrative complexity at forty: Steps toward resolving the scoring dilemma. *Political Psychology, 35*(5), 597–601.

Thoroughgood, C. N., & Sawyer, K. B. (2017). Who wants to follow the leader? Using personality and work value profiles to predict preferences for charismatic, ideological, and pragmatic styles of leading. *Journal of Business and Psychology, 33*, 181–202.

Thoroughgood, C. N., Sawyer, K. B., &Baldock, Z. C. (2020). What About the Followers?: A Preliminary Exploration into the Role of Followers in the Charismatic, Ideological, and Pragmatic Model of Leadership. In *Extending the Charismatic, Ideological, and Pragmatic Approach to Leadership* (pp. 225–253). New York: Routledge.

Tsai, K. C. (2017). Development of the teacher leadership style scale. *Social Behavior and Personality, 45*(3), 477–490.

Uhl-Bien, M., Riggio, R. E., Lowe, K. B., & Carsten, M. K. (2014). Followership theory: A review and research agenda. *The Leadership Quarterly, 25*(1), 83–104.

Van Knippenberg, D., & Sitkin, S. B. (2013). A critical assessment of charismatic – transformational leadership research: Back to the drawing board? *The Academy of Management Annals, 7*(1), 1–60.

Vecchio, R. P., Justin, J. E., & Pearce, C. L. (2008). The utility of transactional and transformational leadership for predicting performance and satisfaction within a path-goal theory framework. *Journal of Occupational and Organizational Psychology, 81*(1), 71–82.

Von Bertalanffy, L. (1950). The theory of open systems in physics and biology. *Science, 111*, 23–29.

Watts, L. L., Ness, A. M., Steele, L. M., & Mumford, M. D. (2018). Learning from stories of leadership: How reading about personalized and socialized politicians impacts performance on an ethical decision-making simulation. *The Leadership Quarterly, 29*, 276–294.

Watts, L. L., Rothstein, E. G., & Patel, K. R. (2020). Multiple pathways to studying outstanding leadership: It is time to expand the methodological toolbox. In S. T. Hunter & J. B. Lovelace (Eds.), *Multiple pathways to outstanding leadership: Revisiting CIP theory* (pp, 48–77). New York: Routledge.

Weber, M. (1924). *The theory of social and economic organizations*. New York: Free Press.

Weber, M. (1947). *The theory of social and economic organizations*. Translated by T. Parsons. New York: Free Press.

Weick, K. E. (1995). *Sensemaking in organizations*. Thousand Oaks: Sage.

Wowak, A. J., Gomez-Mejia, L. R., & Steinbach, A. L. (2017). Inducements and motives at the top: A holistic perspective on the drivers of executive behavior. *Academy of Management Annals, 11*(2), 669–702.

Wren, D. A., & Bedeian, A. G. (2020). *The evolution of management thought*. New York: John Wiley.

Yukl, G. (1998). *Leadership in organizations*. Englewood Cliffs: Prentice Hall.

Yukl, G. (1999). An evaluation of conceptual weaknesses in transformational and charismatic leadership theories. *The Leadership Quarterly, 10*(2), 285–305.

Yukl, G., & Gardner, W. L. (2020). *Leadership in organizations* (9th ed.). Harlow: Pearson.

Yukl, G., Gordon, A., & Taber, T. (2002). A hierarchical taxonomy of leadership behavior: Integrating a half century of behavior research. *Journal of Leadership & Organizational Studies, 9*(1), 15–32.

Zaccaro, S. J. (2007). Trait-based perspectives of leadership. *American Psychologist, 62*(1), 6–16.

Zaccaro, S. J., Green, J. P., Dubrow, S., & Kolze, M. (2018). Leader individual differences, situational parameters, and leadership outcomes: A comprehensive review and integration. *The Leadership Quarterly, 29*(1), 2–43.

Zhou, J., & George, J. M. (2003). Awakening employee creativity: The role of leader emotional intelligence. *The Leadership Quarterly, 14*(4–5), 545–568.

Cambridge Elements ≡

Leadership

Ronald Riggio
Claremont McKenna College

Ronald E. Riggio, Ph.D. is the Henry R. Kravis Professor of Leadership and Organisational Psychology and former Director of the Kravis Leadership Institute at Claremont McKenna College. Dr. Riggio is a psychologist and leadership scholar with over a dozen authored or edited books and more than 150 articles/book chapters. He has worked as a consultant and serves on multiple editorial boards.

Susan Murphy
University of Edinburgh

Susan E. Murphy is Chair in Leadership Development at the University of Edinburgh Business School. She has published numerous articles and book chapters on leadership, leadership development, and mentoring. Susan was formerly Director of the School of Strategic Leadership Studies at James Madison University and Professor of Leadership Studies. Prior to that, she served as faculty and associate director of the Henry R. Kravis Leadership Institute at Claremont McKenna College. She also serves on the editorial board of *The Leadership Quarterly*.

Georgia Sorenson
University of Cambridge

The late Georgia Sorenson, Ph.D., was the James MacGregor Burns Leadership Scholar at the Moller Institute and Moller By-Fellow of Churchill College at Cambridge University. Before coming to Cambridge, she founded the James MacGregor Burns Academy of Leadership at the University of Maryland, where she was Distinguished Research Professor. An architect of the leadership studies field, Dr. Sorenson has authored numerous books and refereed journal articles.

About the Series

Cambridge Elements in Leadership is multi- and inter-disciplinary, and will have broad appeal for leadership courses in Schools of Business, Education, Engineering, Public Policy, and in the Social Sciences and Humanities.

Cambridge Elements ≡

Leadership

Elements in the Series

A full series listing is available at: www.cambridge.org/CELE

Printed in the United States
by Baker & Taylor Publisher Services